Anonymous

Medals of the Roman Pontiffs

From Martin v., 1417, to Pius IX., 1870

Anonymous

Medals of the Roman Pontiffs
From Martin v., 1417, to Pius IX., 1870

ISBN/EAN: 9783337042547

Printed in Europe, USA, Canada, Australia, Japan

Cover: Foto ©ninafisch / pixelio.de

More available books at **www.hansebooks.com**

MEDALS

OF THE

...AN PONT...

FROM

...N V., 1417, TO PIUS IX...

...COINED AT THE ROMAN MINT.

...TING SOME OF THE PRINCIPAL
...HEIR RESPECTIVE PONTIFICATE...

...LATED FROM THE ITALIAN CATA...

PHILADELPHIA:
1882.

PHILADELPHIA:
1882.

INDEX.

Martin V.,	. . . .	1417–1431.	Leo XI., ...	1605.
Eugene IV.,	. . .	1431–1447.	Paul V., ...	1605–1621.
Nicholas V.,	. . .	1447–1455.	Greg. XV., ...	1621–1623.
Callixtus III.,	. . .	1455–1458.	Urban VIII., . . .	1623–1644.
Pius II.,	. . . . .	1458–1464.	Innoc. X., ...	1644–1655.
Paul II.,	. . . . .	1464–1471.	Alex., VII., . . .	1655–1667.
Sextus IV.,	. . . .	1471–1484.	Clem. IX., ...	1667–1669.
Innoc. VIII.,	. . .	1484–1492.	Clem. X., ...	1670–1676.
Alex. VI.,	. . . .	1492–1503.	Innoc. XI., ...	1676–1689.
Pius III.,	. . . .	1503.	Alex. VIII., . . .	1689–1691.
Julius II.,	. . . .	1503–1518.	Innoc. XII., . . .	1691–1700.
Leo X.,	. . . . .	1518–1521.	Clem. XI., ...	1700–1721.
Adrian VI.,	. . .	1522–1523.	Innoc., XIII., . . .	1721–1724.
Clem. VII.,	. . .	1523–1534.	Bened. XIII., . . .	1724–1730.
Paul III.,	. . . .	1534–1549.	Clem. XII., ...	1730–1740.
Julius III.,	. . . .	1550–1555.	Bened. XIV., . . .	1740–1758.
Marcellus II.,	. . .	1555.	Clem. XIII., . . .	1758–1769.
Paul IV.,	. . . .	1555–1559.	Clem. XIV., . . .	1769–1774.
Pius IV.,	. . . .	1559–1565.	Pius VI., ...	1775–1799.
St. Pius V.,	. . .	1566–1572.	Pius VII., ...	1800–1823.
Greg. XIII.,	. . .	1572–1585.	Leo XII., ...	1823–1829.
Sextus V.,	. . . .	1585–1590.	Pius VIII., ...	1829–1830.
Urban VII.,	. . .	1590.	Greg. XVI., . . .	1831–1846.
Greg. XIV.,	. . .	1590–1591.	Pius IX., ...	1846–1878.
Innoc. IX., ...		1591.		Medals to 1870.
Clem. VII.,	. . . .	1592–1605.	Leo XIII., ...	1878–None.

MEDALS OF THE ROMAN PONTIFFS.

MARTIN V. 1417 to 1431.

1. First year of his Pontificate.
  ROMA. MCDXVII.

2. The New Pope enthroned.
  ROMÆ.

3. Martin the Fifth restored and embellished many of the Roman basilicas.
  DIRUTAS. AC. LABANTES. URBIS. RESTAUR. ECCLES.
  On the reverse
  COLUMNA. HUJUS. FIRMA. PETRA.

4. Celebration of the jubilee.
  On the reverse
  INTRABUNT. JUSTI. PER. EAM.

EUGENIUS IV. 1431 to 1447.

5. The newly elected Pope enthroned.
  QUEM. CREANT. ADORANT.
  On the reverse
  ROMÆ.

6. Canonization of St. Nicholas of Tolentino.
>   NICOLAI. TOLENTENATIS. SANCTITAS. CELEBRIS. REDDITUR.
>   On the reverse
>   SIC. TRIUMPHANT. ELECTI.

7. Justice with the scales.
>   REDDE. CUIQUE. SUUM.

NICHOLAS V.   1447 to 1455.

8. Arms of the Pope.
>   THOMAS. LUGANO. DI. SARZANA.

9. Porta Santa closed, with rays.
>   ANNO. JUBIL. ALMA. ROMA.

10. Cross with two palms and the crown of thorns.
>   VICTRIX. CASTA. FIDES.

PONTIFICATE OF CALLISTUS III.   1455 to 1458.

11. Naval expedition against the Turks.
>   HOC. VOVI. DEO.
>   On the reverse
>   UT. FIDEI. HOSTES. PERDEREM. ELEXIT. ME.

12. The walls of Rome fortified.
>   On the reverse
>   NE. MULTORUM. SUBRUATUR. SECURITAS.

13. The cross on the mount.   Tiara above.
>   OMNES. REGES. SERVIENT. EI.

PONTIFICATE OF PIUS II. 1458 to 1464.

14. GLORIA. SINENSI. D. C. PICCOLOMINI.
Arms of the family.
VELOCITER. SCRIBENTIS. SOBOLES.
On the reverse
NE. TANTI. ECCLESIÆ. PACISQ. AMANTIS
DELEATUR. MEMORIA.
IMPOSITA. TURCARUM. LEX.

15. Inscription, etc., the same as above.
VELOCITER. SCRIBENTIS. SOBOLES.
Alludes to the many works written by this Pontiff.

16. OPTIMO. PRINCIPI.
In memory of the distinguished qualities of this Pontiff.

PAUL II. 1464 to 1471.

17. ANNO. MCDLXIV.
On the reverse
ROMA.

18. ANNO. CHRISTI. MCCCCLXX. HAS. ÆDES.
CONDIDIT.
Building of the great palace near St. Mark.

19. SOLUM. IN. FERAS. PIUS. BELLATUR. PASTOR.
The zeal of this Pontiff in extirpating heresy.

20. HILARITAS. PUBLICA.
The pacification of Italy.

SIXTUS IV. 1471 to 1484.

21.
ETSI. ANNOSA. GERMINAT.
Arms of the Pontiff with the tiara and keys.

22.
CITA. APERITIO. BREVES. ÆTERNAT. DIES.
Opening of the Porta Santa.

23.
ANNO. JUBIL. ALMA. ROMA.
On the reverse
1475.

24.
CONSTITUIT. EUM. DOMINUM. DOMUS. SUÆ.
On the reverse
ROMA.
Closing of the Porta Santa.

INNOCENT VIII. 1484 to 1492.

25.
INNOCENTIUS VIII. PONT. MAX.
ANNO. DOMINI. MCDLXXXIV.

26.
ECCE. SIC. BENEDICETUR. HOMO.
On the reverse
ROMA.

ALEXANDER VI. 1492 to 1503.

27.
ALESSANDRO VI. PONT. MAX.
RODERICO. LENZUOLA. D. BORGIA. MCDXCII.

28.
CITA. APERITIO. BREVES. AETERNAT. DIES.
Opening of the Porta Santa.

29.
    RESERAVIT. ET. CLAUSIT. ANN. JUB.
       Closing of the Porta Santa.

PIUS III. 1503.

GLORIA. SENNENSI. D. C. PICCOLOMINI.
30. Arms of the Pontiff.

31.   SUB. UMBRA. ALARUM. TUARUM.
   On the reverse
          MDIII.

JULIUS II. 1503 to 1518.

32.
    JULIUS. LIGUR. PAPA. SECUNDUS.
      ETSI. ANNOSA. GERMINAT.
        With the family oak.

33.   JULIUS. LIGUR. PAPA. SECUNDUS.
        VATICANA. MONS.
The Vatican Temple according to the design of Bramante.

34.
        ANNONA. PUBLICA.
The care of the Pontiff in providing Rome with grain during the famine of 1505.

35.
    JULIUS. LIGUR. PAPA. SECUNDUS.
      PORTUS. CENTUMCELLÆ.
The fortress and port of Civitavecchia with ships.

36.   JULIUS. LIGUR. PAPA. SECUNDUS.
The same as No. 35, larger size.

37.   JULIUS. LIGUR. PAPA. SECUNDUS.
TEMPLUM. VIRG. LAURETI.
On the reverse
MDVIII.
View of the Sanctuary of Loreto.

LEO X. 1518 to 1521.

38   LEO X. PONTIFEX. MAX.
GLORIA. ET. HONORE. CORONASTI. EUM.
Arms of the house of Medici.

39.   LIBERALITAS. PONTIFICIA.
Munificent patron of the arts.

40.   LEO. X. PONTIFEX. MAX.
Same as No. 39, of smaller size.

ADRIAN VI. 1522 to 1523.

41.   ADRIANUS. VI. PONT. MAXIM.
QUEM. CREANT. ADORANT.
On the reverse
ROMÆ.

42.   SPIRITUS. SAPIENTIÆ.
On the reverse
ROMÆ.
Alludes to the learning of the Pontiff.

43.   ADRIANUS VI. PONT. MAX.
The same as No. 42, smaller size.

44. ADRIANUS VI. PONT. MAX.
S. PETRUS S. PAULUS. ROMA.
Two small figures of the Apostles in the niche.

CLEMENT VII. 1523 to 1534.

45. CLEMENS VII. PONT. MAX.
Underneath
MDXXV AN.II.
GLORIA. ET. HONORE. CORONASTI. EUM. ROMA.
Arms of the house of Medici.

46. RESERAVIT. ET. CLAUSIT. ANN. JUB.
Pope assisted by the clergy closes the Porta Santa.

47. CLEM. VII. PONT. MAX.
EGO. SUM. JOSEPH. FRATER. VESTER.
Attachment of the Pontiff to the Florentines.
This medal was much esteemed by Bonanni, Venuti and others and is attributed to Benvenuto Cellini.

PAUL III. 1534 to 1549.

48. PAULUS. III. PONT. MAX. AN. XV.
MDIL.
AVITÆ FARNESIORUM STIRPIS.
Arms of the house of Farnesi.

49. PAULUS III. PONT. MAX. AN. XVI.
On the reverse
ALMA ROMA.
View of the City of Rome.

50.   PAULUS III. PONT. MAX. AN. XVI.
                ANNONA. PONT.

51. PAULUS TERTIUS PONT. OPT. MAX. ANNO XVI.
        HARUM ÆDIDIUM FUNDATOR.
            View of the Farnesi Palace.

52.   PAULUS III. PONT. MAX. ANNO. XVI.
    Opening of the Porta Santa. Greek characters. Much
        praised by Bonanni, Venuti, and others.

53. PAULUS. TERTIUS. PONT. MAX. ANNO. XVI.
                RUFINA.
            TUSCOLO. REST.
    View of Frascati and the Villa Rufina.

54. Inscription, etc., same as above.
        IN. VIRTUTE. TUA. SERVATI. SUMUS.
    The liberation of Corfu from the siege of the Turks. This
        medal, according to Bonanni and Venuti is very rare.

            JULIUS III.   1550 to 1555.

55. JULIUS III. PONT. MAX. ANNO JUBILEI MDL.
    On the reverse
            PETRO. APOST. PRINC.
    Facade of the Vatican Basilica according to the design of
        San Gallo.

56. The same of larger size.

57. Inscription, etc., same as above.
            HÆC. PORTA. DOMINI. MDL.
    On the reverse
                ROMA
    Porta Santa.   JUSTI. INTRABUNT. PER. EAM.

75. Inscription, etc., same as above.

    Christ disputing with the Doctors.

PAUL IV. 1555 to 1559.

76.   PAULUS. IIII. PONT. OPT. MAX.

On the reverse

    CLAVES. REGNI. CELOR.

St. Peter receives the Keys from Christ.

77. Inscription, etc., same as above.

On the reverse

    ROMA. RESURGENS.

Armed figure of Rome, believed to signify the peace made between this Pope and Philip II of Spain.

78. Inscription, etc., same as above.

On the reverse

    DOMUS. MEA. DOMUS. ORATIONIS. VOC.

Christ drives the sellers from the Temple.

79.   PAULUS. IV. PONT. MAX. AN. V.
    I. F. P.

On the reverse

    DOMUS. MEA. DOMUS. OR.

80.   PAULUS. IIII. PONT. OPT. M.

    Bust of the Saviour.

81. Inscription, etc., same as above.

On the reverse

    BEATI. QUI. CUSTODIUNT. VIAS. MEAS.

Bust of our Saviour, with nimbus.

82. Inscription, etc., same as above.
   On the reverse
   IN. FLUCTIB. EMERGENS.
   The bark of St. Peter tossed by the waves.

PIUS IV.   1559 to 1565.

83.   PIUS. IIII. PONT. MAX.
   On the reverse
                  INSTAURATA.
   View of the fortress of Castle S. Angelo.

84. Inscription, etc., same as above.
   On the reverse
                  ROMA. RESURGENS.
   Rome armed, signifying her hopes in this Pontiff.

85.   PIUS. IIII. PONTIFEX. MAXIMUS.
   On the reverse
   DIVÆ. CATHARINÆ. TEMPLUM. ANNO. CHRISTI.
                  MDLXI.
   Façade of the church of St. Catharine completed by Pius IV.

86. Inscription, etc., same as above.
   On the reverse
                  PAX.

87. Inscription, etc., same as above.
   On the reverse
            SECURITAS. POPULI. ROMANI.
   Alludes to the fortifications of Castle St. Angelo and Civitavecchia.

88. Inscription, etc., same as above.
>MENDICIS. IN. PTOCHOTROPHIUM. REDACTIS.
>Figure of Charity. Alludes to the hospital of the poor and lunatics founded by this Pontiff.

89. Inscription, etc., same as above.
>DISCITE. JUSTITIAM. MONITI.
>Figure of Justice with the scales and sword.

90. Inscription, etc., same as above.
>VIRGO. TUA. GLORIA. PARTUS.
>Small figure of the *Bl. Virgin* with INFANT JESUS.

91. Inscription, etc., same as above.
>NE. DETERIUS. VOBIS. CONTINGAT.
>The Pope blesses the people.

92. Inscription, etc., same as above.
>CLAVES. REGNI. CELOR.
>On the reverse
>>ROMA.
>
>Our Lord gives the keys to St. Peter.

93. Inscription, etc., same as above.
>On the reverse
>>DOMUS. MEA. DOMUS. ORATIONIS. VOC.
>
>Christ drives those who bought and sold from the temple.

PIUS V. 1566 to 1572.

94. PIUS. V. PONTIFEX. MAXIMUS. AN. V.
>A. DOMINO. FACTUM. EST. ISTUD.
>The naval expedition against the Turks.

95. Inscription, etc., same as above.
FŒDERIS. IN. TURCAS. SANCTIO.
Three figures—the Church, the kingdom of Spain, and the republic of Venice.
On the reverse
The lamb, the eagle, and the lion of St. Mark.

96. PIUS. V. PONT. OPT. MAX. ANNO. VI.
DEXTERA TUA. DOM PERCUSSIT INIMICUM, 1571.
The celebrated naval victory over the Turks at Lepanto.

97. Inscription, etc., same as above.
ILLUMINARE. HIER.
On the reverse
PIUS. V. P. M.
The Blessed Virgin with the Infant Jesus. St. Joseph. The three kings adore our Lord.

98. PIUS V. PONTIFEX. MAX.
E. TENEBRIS. DIES. E. LUCO. LUX. LUCET.
A temple in the midst of a grove alludes to the birthplace of the Pontiff, which was Bosco (a grove).

99. 1566.
PIUS. V. GHISLIERIUS. BOSCHEN. PONT. MAX. ECCLESIAM. S. CRUCIS. ORDINI. PRÆDIC. ALLUNNO. SUO. AC. PATRIÆ. ERIGENDAM. CURAVIT. DOTAVITQ.

100. Inscription, etc., same as above.
BOSCHEN. SANCTÆ. CRUCIS. ORDINIS. PRÆDICA TORUM.
On the reverse
MDLXXI.
View of the Church of the Holy Cross in Bosco.

101. Inscription, etc., same as above.
PAX.
The figure of *Peace* in front of a church.

102. Inscription, etc., same as above.
CLAVES. REGNI. CELOR.
Our Lord gives the keys to St. Peter.

103. Inscription, etc., same as above.
IN FLUTIB. EMERGENS.
The bark of St. Peter.

104. Inscription, etc., same as above.
On the reverse
DOMUS. MEA. DOMUS. ORATIONIS. VOC.
Our Lord drives from the temple those who bought and sold.

105. Inscription, etc., same as above.
IMPERA. DMNE. ET FAC. TRANQUILLITATEM.
The apostles beg our Lord to calm the tempest.

106.   PIUS. V. PONTIFEX. MAX. A. VI.
BEATI. QUI. CUSTVDIUNT. VIAS. MEAS.
Bust of our Lord, with the halo.

107. Inscription, etc., same as above, but larger.

108. Inscription, etc., same as above.
DOMINE QUIS SIMILIS TIBI.
The bust of our Saviour.

109. PIUS. V. GHISLERIUS. BOSCHEN. PONT. M.
MILITANS. DE. INFERO. TRIUMPHAT. ECCLESIA.
On the reverse
PONTIFICIÆ. POTESTATIS. IMPERIUM.
A person possessed, liberated from the evil spirits by this holy Pontiff.

GREGORY XIII. 1572 to 1585.

110.   GREGORIUS XIII. PONT. MAX. AN. I.
          UGONOTTORUM. STRAGES. 1572.
    Alludes to the slaughter on St. Bartholomew's Day.

111. Inscription, etc., same as above.
          CLAVES. REGNI. CELOR.
  On the reverse
          ROMA.
  Our Lord gives the keys to St. Peter.

112. Inscription, etc., same as above.
          IN. FLUCT. EMERGENS.
  The bark of St. Peter with the apostles.

113. Inscription, etc., same as above.
          PROVIDENTIA. CHRISTI.
  Figure of the Providence of God.

114. Inscription, etc., same as above.
          VIRGO. TUA. GLORIA. PARTUS.
  The Blessed Virgin with the Infant Jesus in her arms.

115. Inscription, etc., same as above.
          DOMUS. DEI. ET. PORTA. CŒLI. 1571.
  Opening of the Porta Santa.

116. Inscription, etc., same as above.
          ET. PORTÆ. CÆLI. APERTÆ. SUNT.
  On the reverse
          ROMA.
  The Porta Santa ornamented with festoons, etc., etc.

117. Inscription, etc., same as above.
GREG. XIII. P. M. APERUIT. ET. CLAUSIT.
On the reverse
A. JUBILÆI. 1575.
The Porta Santa closed by this Pontiff.

118. Inscription, etc., same as above.
APERUIT. ET. CLAUSIT. ANNO. MDLXXV.
On the reverse
ROMA.
The Porta Santa closed.

119. Inscription, etc., same as above.
ET. IN. NATIONES. GRATIA. SPIRITUS. SANCTI.
St. Peter preaching.

120. Inscription, etc., same as above.
SUPER. HANC. PETRAM.
On the reverse
ROMA.
View of St. Peter's, Rome.

121. Inscription, etc., same as above.
GREGORIANA. D. NATZIANZANO. DICATA.
View of the Gregorian chapel in St. Peter's, Rome.

122. Inscription, etc., same as above.
ANNONA. PONT.
Two figures and a beautiful ship.

123. Inscription, etc., same as above.
BEATI. QUI. CUSTODIUNT. VIAS. MEAS.
Bust of our Saviour, with halo.

124. Inscription, etc., same as above.
>TUTUM. REGIMEN.
On the reverse
>ROMA.

Fortifications made by the Pontiff to defend the sea coast of the Pope's States from the Corsairs.

125. Inscription, etc., same as above.
>VERUS. DEI. CULTUS.

The Church with a tablet on which is written S. ROM. EC.

126. Inscription, etc., same as above.
>SECURITAS. POPULI. ROMANI.

Figure of "Safety."

127. Inscription, etc., same as above.
>VIATORUM. SALUTI. ANN. DNI. MDLXXX.

Bridge of six arches over the river Palia, near to Aqua Pendente.

128. Inscription, etc., same as above.
>UT. FAMULU. TUU. GREG. CONSERVARE. DIGNE.
On the reverse
>1582.

Front of the Church of the "Madonna dei Monti."

129. Inscription, etc., same as above.
>PORTUS. CENTUMCELL. INSTAUR. URBEQ. VALLO. DUXIT.

View of the port of Civitavecchia.

130. Inscription, etc., same as above.
>ANNO. RESTITUTO. MDLXXXII.

Emendation of the calendar made by this Pontiff.

131. Inscription, etc., same as above.
AB. REGIBUS. JAPONIOR. PRIMA. AD. ROM. PONT. LEGATIO. ET OBEDIENTIA. 1585.
Alludes to the embassy sent to the Pontiff by three princes of Japan.

132. Inscription, etc., same as above.
MENDICIS. IN. PTOCHOTROPHIUM. REDACTIS.
The figure of "Charity," with four children.

SIXTUS V. 1585 to 1590.

133. SIXTUS. V. PONTIFEX. MAX. ANN. I.
PIUS. V. PONTIFEX. MAX.
Portrait of St. Pius V.

134. Inscription, etc., same as above.
DOMUS. MEA. DOMUS. ORATIONIS. VOC.
Our Lord drives from the temple the buyers and sellers.

135. Inscription, etc., same as above.
IN. FLUCT. EMERGENS.
The bark of St. Peter with the apostles.

136. Inscription, etc., same as above.
TUTUM REGIMEN.
On the reverse
ROMA.
Figure of Rome, with helmet.

137. Inscription, etc., same as above.
BEATI. QUI. CUSTODIUNT. VIAS. MEAS.
Bust of our Saviour, with halo.

138. Inscription, etc., same as above.
CURA. PONTIFICIA.
Four streets which start from the Church of St. Mary Major.

139. Inscription, etc., same as above.
EXULTAVIT. HUMILES. 1587.
The statues of SS. Peter and Paul placed on the Trajan and Antonine columns.

140. Inscription, etc., same as above.
TERRA. MARIQUE. SECURITAS. 1588.
Five galleys armed by the Pontiff.

141. Inscription, etc., same as above.
PERFECTA. SECURITAS.
Alludes to the care of the Pontiff in liberating the Ecclesiastical States from assassins.

142. SIXTUS. V. P. MAX. AD. BENEDICTIONES. A. V.
Small figure of the Pope in the act of blesssing.
The reverse has no impression on it.

143. Inscription, etc., same as above.
SECURITAS. POPULI. ROMANI.
The figure of "Safety," with the sceptre in her left hand.

144. Inscription, etc., same as above.
CRUCE. FELICIUS. CONSECRATA.
The four obelisks—Popolo, Vatican, Lateran, and that near St. Mary Major, erected by this Pope.

145. Inscription, etc., same as above.
MEM. FL. CONSTANT. RESTITUTA.
The two colossal equine statues on the Quirinal.
OPUS. PHID. OPUS. PRAX.

146. Inscription, etc., same as above.
SUPER HANC PETRAM.
On the reverse
ROMA.
View of St. Peter's, Rome.

URBAN VII. 1590.

147. URBANUS. VII. PONT. MAX. ANNO. I. MDLXXXX.
SIC. LUCEAT. LUX. VESTRA..
The famous "candelabrum" of the Jewish temple.

148. Inscription, etc., same as above.
SPONSUM. MEUM. DECORAVIT. CORONA.
The Church, with "tiara" in right and cross in the left hand.

149. Inscription, etc., same as above.
JUSTITIA. ET. CLEMENTIA. COMPLEXÆ. SUNT. SE.
"Justice" and "Clemency" embrace.

150. Inscription, etc., same as above.
DEXTERA. DOMINI. FACIAT. VIRTUTEM.
The Pope delivers the standard of the Church to a kneeling figure.

GREGORY XIV. 1590 to 1591.

151. GREGORIUS. XIV. PON. MAX.
The arms of the Pope with the tiara and keys.

152.   GREGORIUS. XIV. PONT. MAX.
SPONSUM. MEUM. DECORAVIT. CORONA. 1590.
> The Church with the tiara in the right and the cross in the left hand.

153. Inscription, etc., same as above.
DEXTERA. DOMINI. FACIAT. VIRTUTEM. 1591.
> The Pope with the tiara and cope gives the standard of the Church to a kneeling figure.

154. Inscription, etc., same as above.
DIEBUS. FAMIS. SATURAB.
> Alludes to the providence of the Pope in the famine when he dispensed from the observance of Lent.

INNOCENT IX. 1591.

155.   INNOCENT IX. PONT. MAX. AN. I,
INNOCENT. IX. PONT. MAX.
> Arms of the pontiff with tiara and keys.

156. Inscription, etc., same as above.
RECTIS. CORDE.
> An Angel sustains the tiara with both hands.

157. Inscription, etc., same as above.
JUSTITIA. ET. PAX. OSCULATÆ. SUNT.
> A garland of flowers with the keys crossed in the middle.

158. Inscription, etc., same as above.
ROMA. RESURGENS.
> Rome with a helmet and armed with a spear and shield.

CLEMENT VIII. 1592 to 1605.

159. CLEMENS VIII. PONT. M. A. II.
CONSECRATIO.
The consecration of the Altar of the " Confession " in St. Peter's 1594.

160. Inscription, etc., same as above.
ANNONA. PUBLICA.
Figure crowned with ears of wheat, with cornucopia in the left hand and ears of wheat in the right.

161. Inscription, etc., same as above.
FERRARIA. RECUPERATA.
View of the city of Ferrara

162. Inscription, etc., same as above.
JUBILÆI. INDICTIO.
On the reverse
AN. MDC.
Publication of the jubilee.

163. Inscription, etc., same as above.
PAX. ET. SALUS. A. DOMINO.
On the reverse
MDCI.
Figure of " Peace" with cross in the right hand, and a torch in the left burning the arms.

164 Inscription, etc., same as above.
SALVE. NOS. DOMINE.
Bark tossed by the winds.
The Apostles wake up our Lord to calm the storm.

165. Inscription, etc., same as above.
VELLINO A. MDC.
Alludes to the widening of the river Vellino, after the design of Fontana.

166. Inscription, etc., same as above.
UNUS. DEUS. UNA. FIDES.
The veiled figure of faith, with the cross and the chalice, looking up to heaven.

LEO XI. 1605.

167. LEO XI. PONT. MAX. ANNO I.
DE. FORTI. DULCEDO.
The body of the lion killed by Samson; from whose mouth issues a swarm of bees—symbolic of the excellent qualities of this Pontiff.

PAUL V. 1605 to 1621.

168. PAULUS. V. P. MAX. A. IV.
COMPLEAT. GLORIA. MARIÆ. DOMUM. ISTAM.
View of the Borghese Chapel in St. Mary Major as yet not finished.

169. Inscription, etc., same as above.
IMPERA. DOMINE. ET. FAC. TRANQUILLITATEM.
The bark of the Apostles tossed by the tempest and our Lord calms the storm.

170. Inscription, etc., same as above.
DE. GENITRICE. SEMPER. VIRGINE.
On the reverse
MCDXII.
View of the Borghese Chapel in St. Mary Major.

171. Inscription, etc., same as above.
>TUI. NOMINIS. GLORIA.

The column taken from the temple of Peace and placed before St. Mary Major's with the statue of the Blessed Virgin.

172. Inscription, etc., same as above.
>IN HONOREM APOST.

On the reverse
>ET. PORTÆ. INFE. NO. PRÆVALEBUNT.

View of St. Peter's with the bell towers.

173. Inscription, etc., same as above.
>TU. DOMINUS. ET. MAGISTER.

Washing of the feet on Holy Thursday.

174. PAULUS V. BURGESIUS. R. P. MAX.
>SACELLUM IN. PAL. QUIRIN.

The great door of the Pauline chapel at the Quirinal.

175. Inscription, etc., same as above, larger size.
>PAULUS V. BURGESUIS. RO. P. MAX.

176. Inscription, etc., same as above.
>PALATII VATICANI PORTA RESTITUTA.

The door of the Vatican under the clock.

177. Inscription, etc., same as above.
>CEPERANI. PONS. SUPER. LIRIM. RESTITUTUS.

A bridge with three arches and with the towers of the fortress on the river Garigliano near Ceprano.

GREGORY XV. 1621 to 1623.

178.   GREGORIUS XV. A. III. 1623.
CAUSA NOSTRÆ LÆTITIÆ.

Small figure of the Blessed Virgin, the Infant Jesus and Clouds.

179. Inscription, etc., same as above.
BEATI QUI CUSTODIUNT VIAS MEAS.

The bust of our Lord, with halo.

180. Inscription, etc., same as above.
PACIS. ET. RELIGIONIS. AMOR.

Alludes to the mediation of the Pope between the Kings of France and Spain.

181. Inscription, etc., same as above.

QUINQUE. BEATIS. CŒLESTES. HONORES. DE-
CERNIT. 1622.

Canonization of St. Ignatius of Loyola, of St. Francis Xavier, St. Philip Neri, St. Isidore Agricola, and St. Theresa.

URBAN VIII. 1623 to 1644.

182.   URBANUS. VIII. PONT. MAX. AN. PONT.
MDCXXII. G. M.

On the reverse

FECIT. MIRABILIA. MAGNA. SOLUS.

The Transfiguration. Alludes to this Pope's election on this feast.

183.   URBANUS. VIII. PONT. MAX. A. II. 1625.
PAX. IN. VIRTUTE. TUA.

A figure with a sword in the right hand and the scales in the left.

184. Inscription, etc., same as above.
    HOMINIBUS. BONÆ. VOLUNTATIS.
The Porta Santa of St. John Lateran opened, through which is seen the veil of St. Veronica.

185. Inscription, etc., same as above.
    AB URBANO. VIII. CANONIZATA.
The Canonization of St. Maria Magdalen di Pazzi.

186. Inscription, etc., same as above.
    RESERAVIT. ET. CLAUSIT. AN. JUB. 1625.
The Porta Santa of St. John Lateran closed.

187. Inscription, etc., same as above.
    RESERAVIT. ET. CLAUSIT.
The Porta Santa closed, and on it is seen the veil of St. Veronica.

188. Inscription, etc., same as above.
    SECURITAS. PUBLICA.
Plan of the fortress Urbano.

189. Inscription, etc., same as above.
    S. PETRI. BASILICA. CONSECRATA.
Cross with rays.

190. Inscription, etc., same as above.
    ORNATO. S.S. PETRI. ET. PAULI. SEPULCHRO.
View of the "Confession" of the holy Apostles in St. Peter's, Rome.

191. Inscription, etc., same as above.
    INSTRUCTA. MUNITA. PERFECTA.
View of the Castle St. Angelo.

192. Inscription, etc., same as above.
   DOMINE. QUIS. SIMILIS. TIBI.
    Bust of our Saviour.

193. Inscription, etc., same as above.
  BEATO. ANDREA. INTER. SANCTOS. RELATO.
   The Canonization of St. Andrew Corsini.

194. Inscription, etc., same as above.
    NUNC. RE. PERFECTO.
  View of the port of Civitavecchia with ships.

195. Inscription, etc., same as above.
   TU DOMINUS ET MAGISTER.
On the reverse
    EXEMPL. DEDI. VOBIS.
  Our Lord washes the feet of the apostles.

196. Inscription, etc., same as above.
   AUCTA. AD. METAURUM. DITIONE.
  Rome, with a helmet, a spear in the right hand; St. Peter's, Rome, in the left.

197. Inscription, etc., same as above.
    TE. MANE. TE. VESPERE.
  The Pope on his knees prays to St. Michael, who is seen in the air upon the clouds, the scales in the right hand and the sword in the left.

198. Inscription, etc., same as above.
   S. PETRI. BASILICA. CONSECRATA.
  The consecration of St. Peter's Church, Rome.

199. Inscription, etc., same as above.
    TE. MANE. TE. VESPERE.
   Differs a little from No. 197.

200. Inscription, etc., same as above.
ORNATO. SS. PETRI. ET. PAULI. SEPULCHRO.
View of the "confession" of the holy apostles in St. Peter's, Rome.

201. Inscription, etc., same as above.
ÆDE. S. BIBIANÆ RESTITUTA ET. ORN.
The front of the church of St. Bibiana.

202. Inscription, etc., same as above.
DENUO. EXÆDIFICATA.
View of the church of St. Caius near the baths of Diocletian.

203. Inscription, etc., same as above.
TU. DOMINUS. ET. MAGISTER. EXEM. DEDI. VOBIS.
Our Lord washes the feet of St. Peter.

204. Inscription, etc., same as above.
ÆDE. EXORNATA. FACIE. RESTITUTA.
The front of the church of St. Anastasia.

205. Inscription, etc., same as above.
ORNATO. CONST. LAVACRO ET INSTAURATO.
A section of the baptistery of Constantine at St. John Lateran.

206. Inscription, etc., same as above.
SUB. URBANO. RECESSU. CONSTRUCTO.
View of the pontifical palace of Castel-Gandolfo, country villa of the Pope.

207. Inscription, etc., same as above.
SALVE. NOS. DOMINE.
The apostles in the bark tossed by the winds.

208. Inscription, etc., same as above.
>   DENUO. EXÆDIFICATA.
>   The church of St. Caius.

209. Inscription, etc., same as above.
>   ASSAGGIUM. GENERALE.
>   Pavilion, with the keys crossed.

210. Inscription, etc., same as above.
>   PACIS. INCOLUMITATI.
>   View of the pontifical armory.

211. Inscription, etc., same as above.
MUNIFICENTIA. ANT. BARBERINI. S. R. E. CARD. CAM. SOCIET. JESU. AN. C. PIE. CELEBRATO. 1639.
>   Medal struck by the Jesuits on the occasion of their first centenary.

212. Inscription, etc., same as above.
>   AD. ÆDIUM. PONTIFICUM. SECURITATEM.
>   Bulwark of the Quirinal palace.

213. Inscription, etc., same as above.
>   TE. MANE. TE. VESPERE.
>   St. Michael places the tiara on the Pope.

214. Inscription, etc., same as above.
>   TE. MANE. TE. VESPERE.
>   St. Michael, the archangel, with the scales in his right and the sword in his left hand.

215. Inscription, etc., same as above.
>   S. PETRUS. PRINCEPS. APOSTOLORUM.
>   Bust of St. Peter, with the keys and a halo.

216. Inscription, etc., same as above.
    FERRI FODINIS APERTIS.
    Workmen in the ironworks of Monteleone.

217. Inscription, etc., same as above.
    UBERIORI. ANNONÆ. COMMODO.
    View of the granaries of Termini.

218. Inscription, etc., same as above.
    ADDITIS. URBI. PROPUGNACULIS.
    View of the walls of Rome near the gate of St. Pancratius.

219. Inscription, etc., same as above.
    S. ELIZABETH. REGINA. LUSITANIA. A. DEO. SANCTIFICATA.
    Canonization of the saint by this Pope.

220. Inscription, etc., same as above.
    AUCTA. AD. METAURUM. DITIONE.
    The figure of Rome with the spear in the right hand and the Church of St. Peter in the left.

221. Inscription, etc., same as above.
    PRUDENTER. PASSUS FORTITER EGIT.
    The figure of "Peace" with an olive branch in the right and a palm in the left.

INNOCENT X. 1644 to 1655.

222. INNOCENTIUS. X. PON. MAX. ANN. I.
    FRUCTUM SUUM DEDIT IN. TEMPORE.
    Two angels kneeling on the clouds adore the cross surrounded with rays.
    The election of the Pontiff took place on the feast of the Exaltation of the Cross.

223. Inscription, etc., same as above.
> TU DOMINUS ET MAGISTER.

On the reverse.
> EXEMP. DEDI. VOBIS.

Our Lord washes the feet of St. Peter.

224. Inscription, etc., same as above.
JUSTITIA. ET. CLEMENTIA COMPLEX.Æ. SUNT. SE.
"Justice" and "Clemency" embrace each other. Each has a spear and a shield.

225. Inscription, etc., same as above.
> FRUCTUM. SUUM. DEDIT. IN. TEMPORE.

Two angels support the cross surrounded with rays.

226. Inscription, etc., same as above.
> DECOR. DOMUS. DOMINI.

Section of the Church of St. John Lateran, before it was repaired.

227. Inscription, etc., same as above.
> VATICANIS SACELLIS INSIGNITIS.

The interior of St. Peter's, at Rome, with the ornaments made by this Pope in the side chapels.

228. Inscription, etc., same as above.
UT. THESAUROS. ANNI SANCTIORIS. TECUM APERIAM.

St. Peter with the keys and the book. Alludes to the publication of the jubilee.

229. Inscription, etc., same as above.
> ÆDIFICAT ET. CUSTODIT.

The palace of the Capitoline Museum.

230. Inscription, etc., same as above.
>FIAT. PAX. IN. VIRTUTE. TUA.
>The Eternal Father blessing the world.

231. Inscription, etc., same as above.
>TU. DOMINUS. ET. MAGISTER.
>Our Lord washes the feet of St. Peter.

232. Inscription, etc., same as above.
>ANNO. JUBIL. MDCL.
>Pilgrims kneeling before the Porta Santa in which is seen the veil of St. Veronica.

233. Inscription, etc., same as above.
>HÆC. PORTA. DOMINI. 1650.
>The Pope enters the Porta Santa with the clergy.

234. Inscription, etc., same as above.
>OSTIUM. CŒLI. APERTUM. IN. TERRIS.
>The Pope with cope and tiara opens the Porta Santa.

235. Inscription, etc., same as above.
>ET. PORTÆ. CŒLI. APERTÆ. SUNT. MDCL.
>The Porta Santa between two olive branches.

236. Inscription, etc., same as above.
>LAUDENT. IN. FORTIS. OPERA. EJUS.
>The Pope, assisted by the clergy, closes the Porta Santa.

237. Inscription, etc., same as above.
>APERUIT. ET. CLAUSIT.
>The Porta Santa closed. Above is seen the Blessed Virgin.

238. Inscription, etc., same as above.
>APERUIT. ET. CLAUSIT. MDCL.
>The Porta Santa closed. There is around it a crown of olives.

239. Inscription, etc., same as above.
APERUIT. ET. CLAUSIT. ANN. JUB.
The Porta Santa closed. Above is seen the Blessed Virgin.

240. Inscription, etc., same as above.
ET. PORTÆ. CŒLI. APERTÆ. SUNT. MDCL.
The Porta Santa above which is seen the Blessed Virgin, and in the middle the veil of St. Veronica.

241. Inscription, etc., same as above.
AGNETI. VIRGINI. ET. MARTYRI. SACRUM.
A crown surrounds the inscription.

242. Inscription, etc., same as above.
ABLUTO. AQUA. VIRGINE. AGONALIUM. CRUORE.
The fountain of the piazza Navona with the Obelisk. Work of Bernini.

243. Inscription, etc., same as above.
REPLEVIT. ORBEM. TERRARUM.
The Holy Ghost surrounded by rays and the crown of olives. Alludes to the condemnation of the propositions of Jansenius.

244. Inscription, etc., same as above.
D. AGNETI. VIRGINI. ET. MART. SACRUM.
View of the church of St. Agnes. Architect Bonomino's work.

245. Inscription, etc., same as above.
UT. THESAUROS ANNI. SANCTIORIS. TECUM. APERIAM.
St. Peter with keys and book.

246. Inscription, etc., same as above.
> FRUCTUM. SUUM. DEDIT. IN. TEMPORE.

Two angels sustain the cross surrounded with rays.

247. Inscription, etc., same as above.
> REPLEVIT. ORBEM. TERRARUM.

The Holy Ghost surrounded with rays within a crown of olives.

248. Inscription, etc., same as above.
> TUX DOMINUS ET MAGISTER.

On the reverse
> EXEMP. DEDI. VOBIS.

Our Lord washes the feet of St. Peter.

ALEXANDER VII. 1655 to 1667.

249. ALEXANDER. VII. PONT. MAX. ANN. I.
> VIVO. EGO. JAM. NON. EGO.

Bust of our Lord.

250. Inscription, etc., same as above.
> JUSTITIA. ET. PAX. OSCULATÆ. SUNT.

"Justice" with the sword, and "Peace" with an olive branch embrace each other.

251. Inscription, etc., same as above.
> FEL. FAUS. Q. INGRES.

Interior view of the Porta del Popolo and the entrance into Rome of Christina the Queen of Sweden.

252. Inscription, etc., same as above, but larger.

253. Inscription, etc., same as above.
ASSAGGIUM. GENERALE. MDCLVI.
Pavilion and keys.

254. Inscription, etc., same as above.
UT. UMBRA. ILLIUS. LIBERARENTUR.
Alludes to the cessation of the pestilence, 1656.

255. Inscription, etc., same as above.
POPULUM. RELIGIONE. TUETUR.
Alludes to the same pestilence.

256. Inscription, etc., same as above.
TU. DOMINUS. ET. MAGISTER.
Our Lord washes the feet of the Apostles.

257. Inscription, etc., same as above.
DIVO. NICOLAO. MYRÆ. EPISC.
Front of the church in Castel-Gandolfo, towards the lake.

258. Inscription, etc., same as above.
DILEXI. DOMINE. DECOREM. DOMUS. TUÆ.
Front of the old church in Castel-Gandolfo.

259. Inscription, etc., same as above.
THOMÆ. ARCH. VALENT. INTER. SANCT. RELATO.
The front of same church towards the piazza.

260. Inscription, etc., same as above.
DA. PACEM. DOMINE. IN. DIEBUS. NOSTRIS.
View of the church of St. Maria della Pace, Rome.

261. Inscription, etc., same as above.
ALEXAN. VII. PONT. MAX. FAMIL. PONTIF. COM-
MOD. ET. PALAT. QUIRIN. ORNAM.
View of the Quirinal palace.

262. Inscription, etc., same as above.
>OMNIS. SAPIENTIA. A. DOMINO.
>The courtyard of the archigymnasium of Rome, constructed by Leo X. Design of Michael Angelo and Borromino.

263. Inscription, etc., same as above.
>NAVALE. CENTUMCEL.
>View of the arsenal at Civitavecchia.

264. Inscription, etc., same as above.
>VIVO. EGO. JAM. NON. EGO.
>Bust of our Lord.

265. Inscription, etc., same as above.
>FUNDAMENTA. EJUS. IN. MONTIBUS. SANCTIS.
>Plan of the Piazza of St. Peter's according to Bernino, and view of one side of portico with fountain.

266. Inscription, etc., same as above.
>FUNDAMENTA. EJUS. IN. MONTIBUS. SANCTIS.
>Same view as in No. 265.

267. Inscription, etc., same as above.
>IMMACULATÆ. VIRGINI. VOT.
>View of St. Maria in Campitelli, Rome. A church built in accordance to vow made by the Roman Senate and people in 1566.

268. Inscription, etc., same as above.
>VIRGINIS. ÆDE. ET. PAULI. HOSPITIO. EXORNATIS.

269. The front of St. Maria in Via Lata.
>Designed by Pietro di Cortona.

270. Inscription, etc., same as above.
>REGIA. AB. AULA. AD. DOMUM. DEI.
>>The "Scala Regia" in the Vatican palace.
>>Designed by Bernino.

271. Inscription, etc., same as above.
>PROCEDAMUS. ET. ADOREMUS. IN. SPIRITU. ET. VERITATE.
>>The Pope in the procession of "Corpus Christi."

272. Inscription, etc., same as above.
>>Slightly different from the preceding.

273. Inscription, etc., same as above.
>BEATO. FRANCISCO. EPISCOPO. INTER. SANCTOS. RELATO.
>>The canonization of St. Frances of Sales in the church of St. Peter's, Rome.

274. Inscription, etc., same as above.
>ÆDIBUS. ŒCONOMIÆ. ET. DISCIPLINÆ. RESTITUTIS.
>>View of the hospital—Spirito Santo.

275. Inscription, etc., same as above.
>FUNDAMENTA. EJUS. IN. MONTIBUS. SANCTIS.
>>View of the piazza Vaticana. By Bernini.

276. Inscription, etc., same as above.
>FUNDAMENTA. EJUS. IN. MONTIBUS. SANCTIS.
>On the reverse
>VATICANI. TEMPLI. AREA. PORTICIBUS. ORNATA.
>>View of the piazza Vaticana, slightly different from preceding.

277. Inscription, etc., same as above.
S. ANDRAÆ. APOSTOLO.
Front of S. Andrea della Valle.   Architect, Rainaldi.

278 Inscription, etc., same as above.
FORMAM. SERVI. ACCIPIENS.
Our Lord washes the feet of his disciples.

CLEMENT IX.   1667 to 1669.

279.   CLEM. IX. P. M. CREAT. XX. JUN. 1667.
CONSTANTIA. SILVERII. AD. IMITAN. PROPOSITA.
The Pope was elected on the feast of St. Silverius Pope.

280. Inscription, etc., same as above.
CONSTANTIA. SILVERII. AD. IMITAN. PROPOSITA.
Slightly differing from the preceding.

281. Inscription, etc., same as above.
DEDIT. INDICA. ROSA. ODOREM. SUAVITATIS. ANNO. MDCLXVIII.
The beatification of St. Rosa of Lima.

282. Inscription, etc., same as above.
ALIIS. NON. SIBI. CLEMENS.
The pelican alludes to the clemency and love of this Pope for his subjects.

283. Inscription, etc., same as above.
TU. DOMINUS. ET. MAGISTER.
Our Lord washes the feet of St. Peter.

284. Inscription, etc., same as above.
IPSE. DOMINUS. POSSESSIO. EJUS.
The Paschal Lamb with two olive branches.

285. Inscription, etc., same as above.
> PROTECTOR. NOSTER.
> St. Peter in the act of blessing.

286. Inscription, etc., same as above.
> TU. DOMINUS. ET. MAGISTER.
> Our Lord washes the feet of St. Peter.

287. Inscription, etc., same as above.
> CLEMENS. FŒDERIS. OPUS.
> "Peace," with an olive branch, and "Clemency," with a dart reversed, tramples under foot the demon of discord.

288. Inscription, etc., same as above.
> PACE. POPULIS. SUIS. A. DOMINO. CONCESSA.
> Refers to the treaties of peace of Aquisgrana between France and Spain through the mediation of the Pope.

289. Inscription, etc., same as above.
> ASSAGGIUM. GENERALE. MDCLXIX.
> Pavilion and keys.

290. Inscription, etc., same as above.
> Similar to the preceding, but smaller.

291. Inscription, etc., same as above.
> ADITUM. ECCLESIÆ. MUNIMEN. ET. DECUS. S. PETRUS. DE. ALCANTARA. S. MARIA. MAGDALENA. DE. PAZZIS.
> Alludes to the canonization of these two saints.

292. Inscription, etc., same as above.
> IN. SPLENDORIBUS. SS. PETRUS. DE. ALCANTARA. ET. MARIA. MAGD. DE. PAZZIS.
> Our Lord stretches his hands over the new saints who are kneeling.

293. Inscription, etc., same as above.
B. B. PETRO DE. ALCANTARA. ET. M. MAGDALEND PAZZIS. INTER. SANCTOS. RELATOS.
A crown surrounds them.

294. Inscription, etc., same as above.
ELIO. PONTE. EXORNATO.
The bridge of St. Angelo ornamented with the statues of Angels, designed by Bernini.

CLEMENT X. 1670 to 1676.

CLEMEMS. X. PONT. MAX.
295. SPIRITU. ORIS. EJUS. OMNIS. VIRTUS. EORUM.
The Holy Ghost surrounded by rays illumines the heavens and the earth.

296. Inscription, etc., same as above.
ROMA. RESURGENS.
St. Peter assisted by St. Paul lifts up Rome who is kneeling.

297. Inscription, etc., same as above.
Similar to the preceding.

298. Inscription, etc., same as above.
TU. DOMINUS. ET. MAGISTER.
Our Lord washes the feet of St. Peter.

299. Inscription, etc., same as above.
CUM. ME. LAUDARENT. SIMUL. ASTRA. MATUTINA.
The Immaculate Conception.

300. Inscription, etc., same as above.
>   TU ES PETRUS ET SUPER HANE PETRAM.
>   EDIFICACO ECCLESIAM MEAM.
>   Our Lord gives the keys to St. Peter.

301. Inscription, etc., same as above.
>   COLLES. FLUENT. MEL. DE. PETRA.
>   On the reverse.
>   S. PETRUS. M.
>   St. Peter Martyr with palm in right hand.
>   The election of this Pope fell on the feast of St. Peter Martyr.

302. Inscription, etc., same as above.
>   TU. DOMINUS. ET. MAGISTER.
>   Our Lord washes the feet of St. Peter.

303. Inscription, etc., same as above.
>   PLENA. EST. OMNIS. TERRA. GLORIA. EORUM.
>   Canonization of five Saints: St. Philip Benitius, St. Cajetan, St. Francis, Borgia, St. Louis Bertrand, St. Rose, of Lima.

304. Inscription, etc., same as above.
>   SOLEM. NOVA. SYDERA. NORUNT.
>   These five Saints. The Holy Ghost with rays.

305. Inscription, etc., same as above.
>   DECUS. EJUS. GLORIA. SANCTORUM.
>   The five preceding Saints adoring the Holy Ghost

306. Inscription, etc., same as above.
>   PLENA. EST. OMNIS. TERRA. GLORIA. EORUM.
>   Refers to the five preceding Saints.

307. Inscription, etc., same as above.
>   DEUS. FUNDAVIT. EAM.
> Exterior view of the "Confession" in St. Mary Major.

308. Inscription, etc., same as above.
>   VIVIFICAT. ET. BEAT.
> Charity of the Romans, 1672.

309. Inscription, etc., same as above.
> CUM. ME. LAUDARENT. SIMUL. ASTRA. MATUTINA.
> Immaculate Conception, 1673.

310. Inscription, etc., same as above.
>   PER. ME. VITA. EXTRA. ME. MORS.
> Figure of "Religion" with the cross.

311. Inscription, etc., same as above.
>   INTERCEDITE. PRO. NOBIS.
> The Holy Apostles, St. Peter and St. Paul.

312. Inscription, etc., same as above.
>   UT. ABUNDANTIUS. HABEANT.
> Refers to the care of the Pope in providing bread in the famine of that year.

313. Inscription, etc., same as above.
>   TURCAR. SIGNA. A. POLONIS. RELATA.
> Alludes to the famous victory over the Turks by John Sobieski, King of Poland.

314. Inscription, etc., same as above.
>   DOMUS. DEI. ET. PORTA. CŒLI.
> Opening of the "Porta Santa."

315. Inscription, etc., same as above.
>APERI. EIS. THESAURUM. TUUM.
>Opening of the " Porta Santa."

316. Inscription, etc., same as above.

317. Inscription, etc., same as above.
>APERUIT. DOMINUS. THESAURUM. SUUM.
>Opening of the " Porta Santa."

318. Inscription, etc., same as above.
>FLUENT. AD. EUM. OMNES. GENTES.
>View of St. Peter's Church, Rome.

319. Inscription, etc., same as above.
>LAUDENT. IN. PORTIS. OPERA. EJUS. 1675.
>Closing of the " Porta Santa."

320. Inscription, etc., same as above.
>BENEDIXIT. FILIIS. IN. TE.
>Closing of the " Porta Santa."

321. Inscription, etc., same as above.
>DOMUS. ALTERIA.
>View of the Palace "Altieri."

322. Inscription, etc., same as above.
>CUNCTIS. PATET. INGRESSUS.

View of Civitasecchia. Diminution of Custom House duties.

323. Inscription, etc., same as above.
>INNOCENS. MANIBUS. ET. MUNDO. CORDE.
>Procession of the Pope in St. Peter's, Rome.

324. Inscription, etc., same as above.
DE. CŒLO. RESPEXIT
Figure of "Justice," the Sword in one hand, the Scales in the other.

325. Inscription, etc., same as above.
FIAT. PAX. IN. VIRTUTE. TUA.
The Holy Ghost with rays. Alludes to the efforts of the Pope to pacificate France and Spain who were involved in a terrible war.

326. Inscription, etc., same as above.
DIVINÆ. NUNCIA. MENTIS.
The Eagle, the Lion, and the Zodiac. Arms of this Pope.

327. Inscription, etc., same as above.
FIAT. PAX. IN. VIRTUTE. TUA.
The Holy Ghost with rays, slightly different from the preceding.

328. Inscription, etc., same as above.
SALVA. NOS. DOMINE.
St. Peter walking on the waves, sustained by our Lord.

329. Inscription, etc., same as above.

330. Inscription, etc., same as above.
AUDITE. VOCES. SUPPLICUM.
The Holy Apostles, St. Peter and St. Paul.

331. Inscription, etc., same as above.
NON. DEFICIET. FIDES. TUA.
The Holy Apostle St. Peter.

332. Inscription, etc., same as above.
UNDE. PENDET.
A crowned figure receives the Scales.

333. Inscription, etc., same as above.
IN. SAECULUM. STABIT.
The figure of "Faith," the Chalice in one hand, the Cross in the other.

334. Inscription, etc., same as above.
IN. DOMINUS. ET. MAGISTER.
Our Lord washes the feet of the Apostles.

335. Inscription, etc., same as above.
FECIT. PACEM. SUPER. TERRAM.
Refers to the celebrated treaty of peace at Nimega.

336. Inscription, etc., same as above.
IN. CŒLO. SEMPER. ASSISTITUR.
St. Michael trampling on the Devil.

337. Inscription, etc., same as above.
NON. QUÆRIT. QUÆ. SUA. SUNT.
The figure of "Charity" with two children.

338. Inscription, etc., same as above.
UNA. SUPER. UNUM.
The figure of the Church with a triple Cross.

339. Inscription, etc., same as above.
IN. SÆCULUM. SHABIT.
The figure of "Religion," with a triple Cross.

340. Inscription, etc., same as above.
IN. DOMINUS. ET. MAGISTER.
Our Lord washes the feet of the Apostles.

— 51 —

341. Inscription, etc., same as above.
DEXTRA. TUA. DOMINE. PERCUSSIT. INIMICUM.
1683.
Refers to the raising of the siege of Vienna by the Turks.

342. Inscription, etc., same as above.
HABETO. NOS. FŒDERATOS. ET. SERVIEMUS. TIBI.
Alludes to the alliance against the Turks between the Pope, the Emperor Leopold, John III, King of Poland, and Mark Anthony Giustiniani, Doge of Venice.

343. Inscription, etc., same as above.
CONFORTAMINI. ET. NON. DISSOLVANTUR. MANUS VESTRÆ.
The Lion of St. Mark at Venice, with sword and torch.

344. Inscription, etc., same as above.
Differs slightly from No. 339.

345. Inscription, etc., same as above.
DOMINUM. FORMIDABUNT. ADVERSARII. EJUS.
The Church, with a cross and torch.

346. Inscription, etc., same as above.
NON. DEFICIET. FIDES. TUA.
The holy apostle, St. Peter, with the keys.

347. Inscription, etc., same as above.
IN. PERPETUUM. CORONATA. TRIUMPHAT.
The cross elevated on a mountain, with the crown of thorns, stands firm against the four winds of heaven.

348. Inscription, etc., same as above.
SPERENT. IN. TE. QUI. NOVERUNT. NOMEN. TUUM.
The figure of "Hope," with the anchor.

349. Inscription, etc., same as above.
>VENITE. ET. VIDETE. OPERA. DOMINI.

A Jesuit missionary presents the ambassador from Tonkin, China, to the Pope.

350. Inscription, etc., same as above.
>FORTITUDO. MEA. DOMINE.

Refers to the war among Christian princes, when James II. was dethroned in England.

ALEXANDER VIII. 1689 to 1691.

351. Alexander VIII., Pont. Max., etc.
>MUNIT. ET. UNIT.

The earth cut by a zone which represents the zodiac.

352. Inscription, etc., same as above.
>SUAVITATE. 1690.

Thurible with incense. Refers to the affability of the Pope, and his skill in ecclesiastical affairs.

353. Inscription, etc., same as above.
>DOMINI. EST. ASSUMPTIO. NOSTRA.

The "chair" of St. Peter, with rays of light.

354. Inscription, etc., same as above.
>Slightly differs from the preceding.

355. Inscription, etc., same as above.
>VICTRICEM. MANUM. TUAM. LAUDEMUS.

Turkish prisoners on the sea-beach. Refers to the victory of the Venetians over the Turks, 1690.

— 53 —

356. Inscription, etc., same as above.
    LAURENTIO. JUST. IN. SS. ALBUM. RELATO.
    Canonization of St. Lawrence Giustiniani.

357. Slightly differs from the preceding.

358. Inscription, etc., same as above.
    Sepulchre of Alexander VIII. in St. Peter's, Rome.

359.
    SEDE. VACANTE. 1691.
    VENI. LUMEN. CORDIUM.
    The Holy Ghost, with rays.

INNOCENT XII. 1691 to 1700.

360.   INNOCENTIUS XII. PONT. MAX.
    A. DEO. DATUS.
    Above, head of a seraph.

361. Inscription, etc., same as above.
    JUSTITIA. ET. ABUNDANTIA. PACIS.
    The figure of " Justice," with the scales and olive branch.

362. Inscription, etc., same as above.
    A. DEO. ET. PRO. DEO.
    The figure of " Charity," with children scattering money.
    Refers to the liberality of the Pope to the poor.

363. Inscription, etc., same as above.
    PACEM. DONES. PROTINUS.
    The Holy Ghost, with rays.

364. Inscription, etc., same as above.
BEATUS. QUI. INTELLIGIT. SUPER. EGENOS. ET. PAUPERES.
The Pope, surrounded by his court, gives audience to the poor.

365. Inscription, etc., same as above.
VIGILAT. QUI. CUSTODIT. EAM.
The holy apostle, St. Peter, with the keys.

366. Inscription, etc., same as above.
ERIT. EGENO. SPES. 1694.
View of the apostolic hospice at "Ripa Grande," on the banks of the Tiber, Rome.

367. Inscription, etc., same as above.
JUSTITIÆ. ET. PIETATI.
View of Monte Citorio, the Court House, Rome.

368. Inscription, etc., same as above.
The front of the church of "S. Maria dei Fornaci," Rome.

369. Inscription, etc., same as above.
QUÆSTUS. MAGNUS. PIETAS. CUM. SUFFICIENTIA.
View of the Basilica Antonina, now the Roman Custom House.

370. Inscription, etc., same as above.
ANNUNTIATE. INTER. GENTES.
The Pope gives the cross to the missionaries of Propaganda.

371. Inscription, etc., same as above.
FUNDAMENTA. FIDEI.
Bust of the holy apostles, St. Peter and St. Paul.

372. Inscription, etc., same as above.
> JUBILEI. SÆCULARIS. INDICTIO. 1700.
> The Porta Santa. JUBILATE DES OMNIS TERRA.

373. Inscription, etc., same as above.
> TU. DOMINUS. ET. MAGISTER.
> Our Lord washes the feet of the apostles.

374. Inscription, etc., same as above.
> SUB. TUUM. PRÆSIDIUM.
> The Blessed Virgin with the infant JESUS.

375. Inscription, etc., same as above.
> INTROITE. PORTAS. EJUS.
> A procession. The "Porta Santa" opened.

376. Inscription, etc., same as above.
> JUSTITIA. ET. ABUNDANTIA. PACIS.
> Figure of "Justice," with the scales and olive branch.

CLEMENT XI. 1700 to 1721.

377. Clemens XI., P. M., 1700.
> REPLEVIT. ORBEM. TERRARUM.
> The Holy Ghost within a crown of olives.

378. Inscription, etc., same as above.
> INFUNDE. LUMEN.
> The Holy Ghost (with rays) illumines the earth.

379. Inscription, etc., same as above.
> PAX. SUPER. ISRAEL.
> Alludes to the ardent zeal of this Pope to make peace among Christian princes.

380. Inscription, etc., same as above.

   FACTUS. EST. PRINCIPATUS. SUPER. HUMERUM. EJUS.

   Our Lord falls under the weight of the cross.

381. Inscription, etc., same as above.

   VADE. ET. PRÆDICA. 1702.

   The Pope sends Cardinal Tournon to China to decide the celebrated controversy concerning the Chinese ceremonies.

382. Inscription, etc., same as above.

   AUXILIUM. MEUM. A. DOMINO.

   View of the church of the Twelve Apostles restored by this Pontiff.

383. Slightly differs from the preceding.

384. Inscription, etc., same as above.

   HAURIETIS. IN. GAUDIO.

   The port of Civitavecchia, with the aqueduct and fountain. Pure water being scarce there, this Pope restored the ancient aqueduct.

385. Inscription, etc., same as above.

   ROBUR. AB. ASTRIS.

   Figure of "Fortitude." Alludes to the constancy of this Pope amid the wars of almost all Europe.

386. Inscription, etc., same as above.

   UT. ERUANTUR. A. VIA. MALA.

   The House of Correction, with the boys who work at the building near the apostolic hospice of St. Michael.

387. Inscription, etc., same as above.
    ADDITO. ANNONÆ. PRÆSIDIO. 1704.
    The granaries of the "Termini" enlarged, with the building near St. Bernard's church.

388. Inscription, etc., same as above.
    COMMODIORI. ANNONÆ. PRÆSIDIA. 1795.
    The granary completed.

389. Inscription, etc., same as above.
    COMMODITATI. ET. ORNAMENTO.
    The new approach of the port on the Tiber at the "Ripetta."

390. Inscription, etc., same as above.
    DEO. SACRA. PESURGERT.
    The machine invented by Fontana to dig up the column of granite near 'Monte Citorio.

391. Inscription, etc., same as above.
    IN. HONOREM. S. CRESCENTII. MARTYRIS.
    The altar of St. Crescentius in the Cathedral S. Urbino, birthplace of this Pope.

392. Inscription, etc., same as above.
    PORTAVERUNT. TABERNACULUM. FŒDERIS.
    1709.
    Procession, with the picture of our most Holy Redeemer in the church of St. John Lateran.

393. Inscription, etc., same as above.
    IN. HONOREM. S. FABIANI. PP. ET. M.
    The family chapel of the "Albani" in the church of St. Sebastian.

394. Inscription, etc., same as above.
> DOMINE. DEPRECABILIS. ESTO.
>> In commemoration of the war in Spain for the succession.

395. Inscription, etc., same as above.
> IN. DOMINUS. ET. MAGISTER.
>> Our Lord washes the feet of St. Peter.

396. Inscription, etc., same as above.
> INTER. SANCTOS. SORS. ILLORUM. 1712.
>> Canonization of St. Pius V., St. Andrew of Avellino, St. Felix of Cantaliccio, and St. Catharine of Bologna.

397. Inscription, etc., same as above.
> ECCLESIA. NOVISG. ÆDIBUS. AD. BALNEA. NUCERINA. CONSTRUCTIS.
>> Above the head of a seraph.

398. Inscription, etc., same as above.
> IN. VIAM. PACIS. 1713.
>> Moses, with the Jews, crosses the Red Sea. Alludes to the peace among Christian princes.

399. Inscription, etc., same as above.
> ECCLESIA. ET. DOMIBUS. AD. BALNEA. NUCERINA. CONSTRUCT. 1714.
>> View of the church of Nocera, and the baths erected by this Pope for the public convenience.

400. Inscription, etc., same as above.
> ARCHICON. SACR. STIGMATUM. S. FRANCISCI.
>> Medal placed by the Pope in the foundations of the church of the Sacred Wounds of St. Francis of Assisium.

401. Inscription, etc., same as above.
TEMPLO. S. CLEMENTIS. INSTAURATO.
View of the church and portico of the church of St. Clement, Rome, restored by this Pontiff.

402. Inscription, etc., same as above.
CORPORE. S. LEONIS. TRANSLATO. 1715.
The remains of the Saint were placed in the chapel which bears his name, in St. Peter's, Rome.

403. Inscription, etc., same as above.
AUXILIUM. CHRISTIANORUM.
The Blessed Virgin of the Rosary; in the distance a fleet. Alludes to the public prayers for the success of the Christian princes over Acmet III., the Turk.

404. Inscription, etc., same as above.
VIRGO. POTENS. ORA. PRO. NOBIS.
The Blessed Virgin with the Divine Infant. Mosaic of Marratta at the "Quirinal."

405. Inscription, etc., same as above.
SUPER. FUNDAMENTUM. APOST. ET. PROPHET.
The Church, radiant, two angels. In the distance St. John of Lateran.

406. Inscription, etc., same as above.
VENTI. ET. MARE. OBEDIUNT. EI.
Our Lord, with the apostles in the bark of St. Peter, calms the storm.

407. Inscription, etc., same as above.
BONARUM. ARTIUM. CULTUI. ET. INCREMENTO.
View of the celebrated institute at Bologna.

408. Inscription, etc., same as above.
ANNO. SALUTIS. 1720. PONT. XX.
Within a crown of olive.

INNOCENT XIII.   1721 to 1724.

409. Innocentius XIII., Pont. Max.
> MICHAEL. ANGEL. DE. COMITIBUS.
> ROMANUS. ELECTUS. 1721.

Medal distributed by the Pope on the occasion of his "possession."

410. Inscription, etc., same as above.
> RENOVABIS. FACIEM. TERRÆ.

The Church reposing on clouds.

411. Slightly differs from the preceding.

412. Inscription, etc., same at above.
> CONSTITUI. TE. PRINCIPEM.

St. Michael trampling the devil under his feet.

413. Inscription, etc., same as above.
> RENOVABIS. FACIEM. TERRÆ.

St. Michael, the Archangel, with sword and shield.

414. Inscription, etc., same as above.
> TU. DOMINUS. ET. MAGISTER.

Our Lord washes the feet of St. Peter.

415. Inscription, etc., same as above.
> OMNIA. POSSUM. IN. EO. QUI. ME. CONFORTAT.

Figure of "Faith," with heavenly rays.

416. Inscription, etc., same as above.
> FRANCISCAN. COMITIIS. SUMMO. PONTIFICE.
> PRÆSIDENTE.

The Pope presides at the general Chapter of the Religions "Minori Osservanti."

BENEDICT XIII. 1724 to 1730.

417. BENEDICTUS XIII. PONT. MAX.
DOMINUS. ILLUMINATIO. MEA.
The famous " Candelabrum" of Jerusalem.

418. Inscription, etc., same as above.
QUID. VOLO. NISI. UT. ACCENDATUR.
St. Dominic in glory with the Angels. In the distance the dog with a lighted torch.

419. Inscription, etc., same as above.
HAURIETIS IN. GAUDIO. DE FONT. SALUTIS.
The figure of " Faith" with Cross and Chalice, 1724.

420. Inscription, etc., same as above.
DE. RORE. CŒLI.
The Rose, the Arms of the Orsini family.

421. Inscription, etc., same as above.
FLUENT. AD. EUM. OMNES. GENTES.
The front of St. Peter's, Rome. The wolf with the twins, Romulus and Remus.

422. Inscription, etc., same as above. ✓
PER. ME. SI. QUIS. INTROIERIT. SALVABITUR.
" Porta Santa" our Lord in the middle. Pilgrims kneeling around.

423. Inscription, etc., same as above.
CAROLO. MAGNO. ROMANÆ. ECCLESIÆ VINDICI
1725.
The Equestrian Statue of Charlemagne, by Agostino Cornacchini Fiorentino in the vestibule of St. Peters, Rome.

424. Inscription, etc., same as above.
ANNO. JUBILEI 1725.
Medal placed in the foundation of the Hospital of St. Gallicano by this Pontiff.

425. Inscription, etc., same as above.
RESERAVIT. ET. CLAUSIT. ANNO. JUB.
Closing of the " Porta Santa."

426. Inscription, etc., same as above.
BEATUS. QUI. INTELLIGIT. SUPER EGENUM.
The Pope in the midst of his Court, receives a number of poor people.

427. Inscription, etc., same as above.
EREXIT. IN. TITULUM.
Jacob anoints the stone, Gen. vi., 28.
Alludes to the Consecration of many Churches, Altars and Sacred Vessels by this Pope.

428. Inscription, etc., same as above.
COR. NOSTRUM. DILATATUM. EST.
View of the Church and Hospital of St. Gallicano completed.

429. Inscription, etc., same as above.
ERGASTULUM. CENTUMCELLENSE
View of the Prison near Corneto.

430. Inscription, etc., same as above.
APOTHEOSIS. IN. LATERANO.
Canonization of St. John Nepomucene.

431. Inscription, etc., same as above.
TU. DOMINUS. ET. MAGISTER.
Our Lord washes the feet of St. Peter.

CLEMENT XII. 1730 to 1740.

432.   CLEMENS XII. PONT. MAX.
LAURENTII. CORSINI. FLORENTINI 1730.
Chalice, tiara and keys.

433. Inscription, etc., same as above.
RECTIS. CORDE. LTÆITIA.
Figure of "Justice," Palm and Scales.

434. Inscription, etc., same as above.
IN. HONOREM. INFANTIS. JESU.
Alludes to the "Bambino Gesu" on the "Exquiline."

435. Inscription, etc., same as above.
PORTÆ. INFERI. NON. PRÆVALEC.
Figure of the "Church," with the Keys in one hand, the Gospel in the other.

436. Inscription, etc., same as above.
ANNO. SALUTIS. 1732.
Refers to the erection of the Chapel in the Vatican in honor of St. Andrew Corsini. Architect Fiorentino Galilei Alessandro.

437. Inscription, etc., same as above.
INSTITIA. FIRMATUR. SOLIUM. 1732.
The arms of Monsignor Trojano Acquaviva, after made Cardinal.

438. Inscription, etc., same as above.
ADJUTOR. IN. OPPORTUNIT.
View of Ancona and the Port.

439. Inscription, etc., same as above.
IN. DOMINUS. ET. MAGISTER.
Our Lord washes the feet of St. Peter.

440. Inscription, etc., same as above.
OB. MEMOR. CHRISTIAN. SECURIT. REST. 1733.
The Arch of Constantine restored.

441. Inscription, etc., same as above.
ADORATE. DOMINUM. IN. ATRIO. SANCTO. EJUS.
View of the front of St. John Lateran; the Portico erected by this Pope.

442. Inscription, etc., same as above.
SACELLO. IN. LATERANEN. BASIL. S. ANDREÆ. CORSINIO. ÆDIFICATO.
Section of the Chapel Corsini in St. John Lateran.

443. Inscription, etc., same as above.
PUBLICÆ. INCOLUMITATIS. PRÆSIDIO.
The "LAZZARETTO" of Ancona. Architect Vanvitelli.

444. Inscription, etc., same as above.
MULTIPLICASTI. MAGNIFICENTIAM.
Alludes to the foundation of the Capitoline Museum.

445. Inscription, etc., same as above.
EX. CONLATICIA. PROBATAQ. MONETA.
Pavilion with the Keys.
ASSAGIUM. GENERALE.

446. Inscription, etc., same as above.
SECURITAS. POPULI. RAVENN. 1735.
A recumbent figure representing Ravenna.

447. Inscription, etc., same as above.
FONTE. AQUÆ. VIRGINIS. ORNATO.
View of the magnificient Fountain of Treves. Architect, Nicolo Salvi Romano.

448. Inscription, etc., same as above.
SACERDOS. MAGNUS. IN. DIEBUS. SUIS. CORROBORAVIT. TEMPLUM.
Medal placed in the foundations of the new Church of the Most Holy name of "Mary."

449. Inscription, etc., same as above.
ADMINISTRORUM. COMMODO. ET. EQUITUM. STATIONIBUS. 1737.
Public Offices of Rome.

450. Inscription, etc., same as above.
ILLOS. ET. GLORIFICAVIT.
The Canonization of St. Vincent de Paul, St. Francis Regis, St. Catharine of Genoa, and St. Julia Falconieri.

451. Inscription, etc., same as above.
PIA. DOMO. SERVATA.
Refers to the liberality of this Pontiff to the Hospital and Houses of "Spirito Santo."

BENEDICT XIV. 1740 to 1758.

452. Benedictus. XIV. Pont. Max.
JUDICABIT. IN. ÆQUITATE. 1740.
Expresses the rare qualities of this Pope, his skill in Law and in ecclesiastical affairs.

453. Inscription, etc., same as above.
TEMPLUM CORROBORAVITET. ATRIUM. EREXIT.
Alludes to the improvements, especially the Portico of St. Mary Major, made by this Pontiff.

454. Inscription, etc., same as above.
        BASIL. LIBER. PORTIC. REST.
    The front of St. Mary Major.   Architect, Ferdinando Fuga.

455. Inscription, etc., same as above.
        UT. MECUM. SIT. ET. MECUM. LABORET.
    Figure of "Divine Providence" holding the Helm.

456. Inscription, etc., same as above.
        VECTIGALIBUS. REMISSIS.
    The Pope makes Civitavecchia a Free Port.

457. Inscription, etc., same as above.
        MEMORIÆ. M. IN. CLEM. BRIT. REGINÆ.
    The sepulchre of Maria Clementina Sobieski, wife of James III, in St. Peter's. Architect, Nicolo Barrigioni. Sculptor, Pietro Bracci.

458. Inscription, etc., same as above.
        EX. PROBATÆ. MONETÆ. SEGMENTIS.
        Pavilion and Keys.
        ASSAGIUM. GENERALE. 1742.

459. Inscription, etc., same as above.
TRICLINII. LEONIANI. PARIETINIS. RESTITUTIS.
The Apsis of the Triclinium near the Lateran Palace.

460. Inscription, etc., same as above.
    VIRTUTI. TROPHOÆ. NOVA. NON. DEGENER. ADDAM.
Alludes to Schools of Design enlarged at the Capitol.

461. Inscription, etc., same as above.
UNIVIT. ET. PALMAMQ. DEDIT.
Canonization of St. Fidelis of Sigmaringa, St. Joseph of Leonessa, St. Camillus de Lellis, St Peter Regalada, and St. Catharine dei Ricci.

462. Inscription, etc., same as above.
PIA. DOMO. SERVATA.
The Pope in the midst of poor children.

463. Inscription, etc., same as above.
CURA. RERUM. PUBLICARUM.
The Pope goes in a common vehicle to " Civitavecchia."

464. Inscription, etc., same as above.
EGO. JUSTITIAS. JUDICABO.
The figure of " Wisdom," with a sceptre, etc.

465. Inscription, etc., same as above.
EX. COLLECTIS. FRAGMENTIS. 1747.
Pavilion and keys.
Assagium Generale.

466. Inscription, etc., same as above.
AMPLIORI. BONARUM. ARTIUM. INCREMENTO.
The Pope founded the picture gallery at the Capitol.

467. Inscription, etc., same as above.
FLUENT. AD. EUM. OMNES. GENTES.
The publication of the Jubilee, 1750.

468. Inscription, etc., same as above.
MDCCL.
Opening of the '"Porta Santa."

469. Inscription, etc., same as above.
INTROITE. PORTAS. EJUS.
Procession through the "Porta Santa."

470. Inscription, etc., same as above.
ET. CLAUSIT.
Closing of the "Porta Santa."

471. Inscription, etc., same as above.
FRANCISCAN. COMITIIS. PRÆSEDIT.
Assists at the General Chapter of the Franciscan Friars.

472. Inscription, etc., same as above.
EGO. JUSTITIAS. JUDICABO.
Figure of "Justice," with the "tiara" and sceptre.

473. Inscription, etc., same as above.
SECURITAS. PUBLICA.
Figure of Public "Safety," 1752.

474. Inscription, etc., same as above.
CONCORDIA. MUTUA.
The "Church," with scales, extends the hand to the Republic of Venice.

475. Inscription, etc., same as above.
NOVO. ECCLESIARUM. FŒDERE.
Two bishops, with double cross, join hands in harmony.

476. Inscription, etc., same as above.
TU. DOMINUS. ET. MAGISTER.
Our Lord washes the feet of St. Peter.

477. Inscription, etc., same as above.
VOTA. PUBLICA.
Alludes to the treaty made by the Pope with the King of Naples, 1765.

478. Inscription, etc., same as above.
> PROVIDENTIA. PONTIFICIS.
> Care and vigilance of the Pope.

479. Inscription, etc., same as above.
> AUCTO. TERRA. MARIQUE. COMMERCIO.
> Abundant crops. Safe navigation.

480. Inscription, etc., same as above.
> PARTHEI. DECORE. AUCTO. ET. RESTITUTO.
> The interior of the Pantheon restored. Architect, Posi.

481. Inscription, etc., same as above.
> EGO. DOMINUS. ET. MAGISTER.
> Our Lord washes the feet of St. Peter.

482. Inscription, etc., same as above.
> FRUCTUM. SUUM. DEDIT. IN. TEMPORE.
> The cross adored by two angels.

483. Inscription, etc., same as above.
> SEDE. VACANTE.
> SPIRITU. ORIS. EJUS.
> The Holy Ghost surrounded with rays.

CLEMENT XIII. 1758 to 1769.

484. Clemens XIII., Pont. Max.
> ORIETUR. IN. DIEBUS. EJUS. 1758.
> Figure of "Justice," with scales, etc.

485. Inscription, etc., same as above.
> DEDIT. PAUPERIBUS.
> Figure of "Charity," which pours out money from the cornucopia.

486. Inscription, etc., same as above.
UT. COMEDANT. PAUPERES. POPULI.
View of the granaries of the "Termini," Rome. Distribution of bread to the poor.

487. Inscription, etc., same as above.
MERCIUM. IMPORTANDARUM. COMMODITATI.
Port of Civitavecchia, with new buildings.

488. Inscription, etc., same as above.
GREGORIO. BARBADICO. S. R. E. CARDINALI. E. EPISC. PATAVINO. IN. ALBUM. BEATOR. RELATO.
A crown of olive.

489. Inscription, etc., same as above.
ADVENTUS. PONTIFICIS. CENTUMCELL.
The Pope reviews the navy at Civitavecchia.

490. Inscription, etc., same as above.
PRIMITIÆ. EX. NOVIS. FODINIS. PROPE. POLINUM. UMBRIÆ. OPPIDUM. 1762.
Refers to the opening of mines in Umbria.

491. Inscription, etc., same as above.
NAVIGATIONE. TYBERIS. RESTITUTA. 1763.
Improvement in the navigation of the Tiber.

492. Inscription, etc., same as above.
CENTUMCELLIS. AMPLIATA. CIVITAS.
View of the Fort and city of Civitavecchia.

493. Inscription, etc., same as above.
CURA. PRINCIPIS. AUCTO. MUSÆO. CAPITOLINO.
Two centaurs placed by this Pope in the Capitol.

494. Inscription, etc., same as above.
> REPENTE. DE. COELO. SALUS.
>
> Figure of the "Church," with a cross.

495. Inscription, etc., same as above.
> PALATIUM. QUIRINALE. NOVO. LATERE. AMPLIATUM.
>
> A building erected by this Pope near the Quirinal Palace.

496. Inscription, etc., same as above.
> TU. DOMINUS. ET. MAGISTER.
>
> Our Lord washes the feet of St. Peter.

497. Inscription, etc., same as above.
> PATIENS. ET. BENIGNA. EST.
>
> Figure of "Charity" with three children.

498. Inscription, etc., same as above.
> DECOR. EJUS. GLORIA. SANCTORUM.
>
> Canonization of six saints. St. John Cantius, St. Joseph Calasanctius, St. Jerome Emiliani, St. Joseph of Cupertino, St. Serano of Ascoli, and St. Jane Frances of Chantal.

499. Inscription, etc., same as above.
> LIBERALITAS. REDUX.
>
> Figure of "Bounty," with cornucopia.

CLEMENT XIV. 1769 to 1774.

500. Clemens XIV., Pontif. Max.
> DEDIT. GLORIAM. IN. LOCO. ISTO.
>
> Front of the church of the Twelve Apostles. Alludes to the order of the "Minori Conventuali," to which the Pope belonged.

501. Inscription, etc., same as above.
ELEVAT. PAUPERES.
A figure holds the fruits of the earth and the fruits of the sea.

502. Inscription, etc., same as above.
FACTUS. EST. PRINCIPATUS. SUPER. HUMERUM. EJUS.
Our Lord carries the cross to Mount Calvary.

503. Inscription, etc., same as above.
TU. DOMINUS. ET. MAGISTER.
Our Lord washes the feet of St. Peter.

504. Inscription, etc., same as above.
REFULSIT. SOL.
Harmony between the Church and Portugal.

505. Inscription, etc., same as above.
LIBERALITATE. SUA.
The addition to the new Clementine Museum at the Vatican.

506. Inscription, etc., same as above.
DEUS. NOVA. FŒDERA. SANCIT.
The baptism of the "Infanta" of Spain.

507. Inscription, etc., same as above.
ARTIBUS. RESTITUTIS.
The liberal arts join hands.   Design of Chevalier Mengs.

508. Inscription, etc., same as above.
FRUCTUM. ATTULIT. IN. PATIENTIA.
A palm tree.

PIUS VI. 1775 to 1799.

509. Pius VI., Pont. Max.
> DIVIS. AUSPICIIS. 1775.
> St. Peter, St. Andrew, St. Pius V., chosen by this Pope as his patrons.

510. Inscription, etc., same as above.
> MDCCLXXV.
> Opening of the "Porta Santa."

511. Inscription, etc., same as above.
> ET. CLAUSIT. 1775.
> The Pope closes the "Porta Santa."

512. Inscription, etc., same as above.
> UT. VOTA. PUBLICA. IMPLERET. NOVI. SACRARII. VATICANI. FUNDAMENTA. JECIT. 1776.

513. Inscription, etc., same as above.
> TUETUR. ET. ORNAT.
> The grand barracks of Civitavecchia.

514. Inscription, etc., same as above.
> OPPIDANIS. SERVATIS.
> View of St. Lawrence "Alle Grotte."

515. Inscription, etc., same as above.
> PORTORIIS. SUBLATIS.
> The figure of "Liberty," who removes the toll-gates.

516. Inscription, etc., same as above.
> PUELLARUM. PIARUM. PARTHENON. 1779.
> View of the conservatory for young women near St. Peter, in Montorio.

517. Inscription, etc., same as above.
ARCEM. IN. FORO. GALLORUM. INSTAURAVIT.
Alludes to the restoration of Fort Urbano.

518. Inscription, etc., same as above.
OFFICINÆ. PISTORIÆ. CENTUMCELLARUM.
The public ovens built in Civitavecchia.

519. Inscription, etc., same as above.
PUERIS. FULGINATIUM. ALENDIS. ET. COERCENDIS.
View of the asylum in Foligno, for boys.

520. Inscription, etc., same as above.
FACTUS. EST. PRINCIPATUS. SUPER. HUMERUM. EJUS.
Our Lord goes to Mount Calvary with the cross on his shoulders.

521. Inscription, etc., same as above.
SACRA. SOLEM. FESTO. DIE. S. P. V. AUGUSTÆ. VINDALIC. ACTA.
St. Pius V. giving his blessing from the altar.

522. Inscription, etc., same as above.
OBELISCUM. RUINIS. MAUSOLEI. AUGUSTALIS. A. TOT. SÆCULIS. OBRUTUM. EFFODI. INSTAURARI. ORNARI. ET. EQUIS. AD. LAXANDUM. FRONTIS. SPATIUM. IN. OBLIQUUM. VERSIS. ERIGI. JUSSIT.
Medal coined in commemoration of the erection of the obelisk in front of the Quirinal palace. Architect, Antinori.

523. Inscription, etc., same as above.
SACRARIUM. BASIL. VATICANÆ. E. FUNDAMEN-
TIS. EXSTRUCTUM.
View of the new sacristy at St. Peter's, Rome.

524. Inscription, etc., same as above.
LAURENTIUS. A. BRUNDUSIO. JOANNA. BONOMIA. M. ANNA. A. JESU. BEATORUM. NUMERO. ADDITÆ.
The three beatified saints on clouds.

525. Inscription, etc., same as above.
PUERIS. ET. PUELLIS. ALIMENTARIS. TIFERNAT. TIBERINOR.
The asylum for boys and girls in the city of Castello.

526. Inscription, etc., same as above.
MORIB. CASTIGAND. JUVANDIS. ARTIB. TRE-JENSES.
View of the academy and prisons of Treja.

527. Inscription, etc., same as above.
GYNECEUM. PUPILLARUM. FABRIANI. EXCI-TATUM.
Front of the asylum for girls in Fabriano.

528. Inscription, etc., same as above.
TU. DOMINUS. ET. MAGISTER.
Our Lord washes the feet of St. Peter.

529. Inscription, etc., same as above.
VIA. ALBAN. VELIT. RESTIT.
The Appian way repaired.

530. Inscription, etc., same as above.
> **TEMPLI. SUBLAC. CONSECRATIO. 1789.**
> The Pope consecrates the church of Subiaco.

531. Inscription, etc., same as above.
> **ANNONÆ. P. R. LIBERTATE. RESTITUTA.**
> Cornucopia, maize, and ears of wheat.

532. Inscription, etc., same as above.
> **AGRO. POMPTIN. COLONIS. REST.**
> The draining of the Pontine marshes.

533. Inscription, etc., same as above.
> **ANIENÆ. NAVICLARIUS. PATERE. JUSSO.**
> In the distance is seen the temple of the Sybill at Tivoli.

534. Inscription, etc., same as above.
> **PORTU. INSTAURATO. URBE. MUNITA.**
> The city of Civitavecchia, crowned with a tower, etc.

535. Inscription, etc., same as above.
> **VELINO. IN. NAR. TERT. EMISSO.**
> Confluence of the rivers Velino and Nera.

536. Inscription, etc., same as above.
> **CLERO. GALLIA. PULSO. HOSPIT. ET. ALIM. PRÆBITA.**
> The Pope receives the priests, refugees from France, in the Revolution of 1793.

PIUS VII. 1800 to 1823.

537.
> PIUS VII. PONT. MAX.
> REFULSIT. SOL.
> The Church of St. Peter's, Rome, illuminated by the sun. Design of Gherardo de Rossi.

538. Inscription, etc., same as above.
    ADVENTUI. OPT. PRINCIPIS.
    The triumphal arch in the "Piazza del Popolo," erected by the Roman senate and people on the return of the Pope from exile.

539. Inscription, etc., same as above.
    Differs slightly from No. 538.

540. Inscription, etc., same as above.
    INEUNTE. PONTIFICATUM. SOLEMNITER,
    The Holy Ghost illumines the tiara and the keys.

541. Inscription, etc., same as above.
    REFULSIT. SOL.
    The sun irradiates the Church of St. Peter, Rome, and the Vatican Palace.

542. Inscription, etc., same as above.
    MONETA. RESTITUTA.
    Refers to the financial system of Cardinal Alexander Lante.

543. Inscription, etc., same as above.
    PROMERCIOR. PRIVILEGIA. ABOLITA.
    Refers to the "Free Trade" granted in 1800 by this Pope "motu proprio."

544. Inscription, etc., same as above.
    CAUSA. NOSTRÆ. LÆTITITIÆ.
    Bust of the Blessed Virgin.

545. Inscription, etc., same as above.
    FUNDAMENTA. FIDEI.
    Busts of the Holy Apostles St Peter and St. Paul.

546. Inscription, etc., same as above.
>   EX. GALLIA. REDEUNTI.
>
> The bridge "Ponte Molle" repaired and restored. Design of Valadier.

547. Inscription, etc., same as above.
>   SALINÆ. TARQUIN. INSTITUTÆ.
>
> Refers to the Salt works opened at Corneto.

548. Inscription, etc., same as above.
>   EGO. DOMINUS. QUI. SANCTIFICO. VOS.
>
> The triangle, symbol of the most Holy Trinity. Canonization of St. Francis Caracciolo, St. Benedict the Moor, black man, St. Hyacinth Mariscotti, St. Coletta, and St. Angela Merici.

549. Inscription, etc., same as above.
>   IN. DOMINUS. ET. MAGISTER.
>
> Our Lord washes the feet of St. Peter.

550. Inscription, etc., same as above.
>
> Differs slightly from the preceding.

551. Inscription, etc., same as above.
>   RENOVATUM. PRODIGIUM.
>
> St. Peter liberated by the Angel from the Prison. The triumphant return of the Pope to his States. 1814 Design of De Rossi.

552. Inscription, etc., same as above.
>   POPULO. CHRISTIANO. PLAUDENTE.
>   PIUS VII. RESTITUTUS.
>
> The Angel surrounded with rays, liberates St. Peter from Prison.

553. Inscription, etc., same as above.
    Differs slightly from the preceding.

554. Inscription, etc., same as above.
    URBI. ET. ORBI. RESTITUTUS.
    Two warriors, with helmets, protect the Pope.

555. Inscription, etc., same as above.
    DEDIT. GLORIAM. IN. LOCO. ISTO.
    "Religion" offers a crown to the Blessed Virgin of Savona, crowned by this Holy Pontiff. Design of "de Rossi."

556. Inscription, etc., same as above.
    ET. DUXIT. VINCTOS. IN. FORTITUDINE.
    The column, symbol of "Fortitude, the anchor of "Hope" and the Olive of "Peace" sustain the family arms of this Pope.

557. Inscription, etc., same as above.
    BONONIA. FERRARIA. ÆMILIA. PICENO, BENEVENTO, FREGILLIS, PONTIFICIÆ. POTESTATI. RESTITUTIS. 1725.
    These six provinces restored to the Pope.

558. Inscription, etc., same as above.
    CONSTANTIA. PRINCIPIS. PROVINCIÆ. RECEPTÆ.
    The "Church" receives an Olive branch from the hands of "Peace."

559. Inscription, etc., same as above.
    MONUMENTORUM. VETERUM. RESTITUTORI.
    The group of Lacoon returned (with other *stolen* monuments) by France.

560. Inscription, etc., same as above.
LEGES. LATÆ. 1818.
The figure of "Justice," with the scales and an Olive branch.

561. Inscription, etc., same as above.
TU. DOMINUS. ET. MAGISTER.
Our Lord washes the feet of St. Peter.

562. Inscription, etc., same as above.
VIIS. ALVEIS. ET. OP. PUBL.
The figure of "Architecture," with Compass and book. Alludes to the Council of Arts established by a "Motu proprio." 1817.

563. Inscription, etc., same as above.
TU. DOMINUS. ET. MAGISTER.
Our Lord washes the feet of St. Peter.

564. Inscription, etc., same as above.
FRANC. I. AUSTR. IMP. IN. QUIRINAL. HOSPES.
The Emperor and Empress of Austria received by the Pope in the Palace of the Quirinal.

565. Inscription, etc., same as above.
ACADEMIIS· ARCHIGYMNASII. ROMANI.
Enclosed in a crown.

566. Inscription, etc., same as above.
TU. DOMINUS. ET. MAGISTER.
Our Lord washes the feet of St. Peter.

567. Inscription, etc., same as above.
S. FRANCISCI. SEPULCHRUM. GLORIOSUM.
The Franciscans assisted by the bishops appointed by the Pope for the recognition of the body of St. Francis in Assisi.

568. Inscription, etc., same as above.

NOVUM. MUSEUM. PIUM.

The new wing of the Vatican Museum, erected by Pius VII. Designed by Raphael Stern.

569. Inscription, etc., same as above.

BENEMERENTI.

In a crown of oak. This medal was distributed by the Pope as a premium to those distinguished in any branch of arts, science and skilled labor.

570. Inscription, etc., same as above.

TU. DOMINUS. ET. MAGISTER.

Our Lord washes the feet of St. Peter.
It is a custom of the popes to coin and distribute these medals on Thursday in Holy Week.

571. Inscription, etc., same as above.

AREA. FLAMINIA. EXORNATA.

The "Piazza del Popolo" ornamented with new buildings. Architect, Guiseppe Valadier.

572. Inscription, etc., same as above.

DE. SALUT. PUB. BENEMERENTI.

Premium medal for those who distinguished themselves in the "Vaccination" ordered with repeated decrees by Cardinal Gonsalvi then Secretary of State, 1822.

573. Pius Sextimus Pontifex Max.

CONSECRATIO. PANNONIÆ. PATRI. PATRIÆ. &c.

On the reverse

PONTIFICATUS. SUI. XXIV.

View of a church in Gran, Hungary.

LEO XII. 1823 to 1829.

574.   Leo XII P. M. An. I.
TU. DOMINUS. ET. MAGISTER.
Washing of the Pilgrims' feet on Holy Thursday.

575. Inscription, etc., same as above.
**ELECT. XXVIII SEPT. MDCCCXXII.
CORON. V. OCT. POSS. XIII JAN.**
Takes Possession (il possesso).

576. Inscription, etc., same as above.
PROSPERE. PROCEDE. ET. REGNA.
Another possession, St. Michael, Archangel.

577. Inscription, etc., same as above.
UT. THESAUROS. ANNI. SANCTIORIS. TECUM. APERIAM.
Publication of the Jubilee.

578. Inscription, etc., same as above.
BENEMERENTI.

579. Inscription, etc., same as above.
BENEMERENTI.
Larger size.

580. Inscription, etc., same as above.
ACADEMIIS. ARCHIGYMNASII. ROMANI.

581. Inscription, etc., same as above.
AUDITORIBUS. ARCHIGYMNASII. ROMANI.

582. Inscription, etc., same as above.
TU. DOMINUS. ET. MAGISTER.
Washing the feet on Holy Thursday.

— 83 —

583. Inscription, etc., same as above.
JANUAS. CŒLI. APERUIT.
Opening of the " Porta Santa."

584. Inscription, etc., same as above.
BASILIC. S. PAULI. EX. INCENDIO.
The destruction of St. Paul's by fire.

585. Inscription, etc., same as above.
SEDET. SUPER. UNIVERSUM.
Figure of " Religion."

586. Inscription, etc., same as above.
ET. CLAUSET. MDCCCXXV.
Closing of the " Porta Santa."

587. Inscription, etc., same as above.
LEO XII. P. M. STUDIORUM. INSTAURATORI.
MISIT. ANCILLAS. SUAS. UT. VOCARENT. AD. ARCEM.
Premium for the congregation of studies.

588. Leo XII., Anno III.
TU. DOMINUS. ET. MAGISTER.
Washing the feet on Holy Thursday.

589. Inscription, etc., same as above.
INFIRMUS. ERAM. ET. VISITASTIS. ME.
Visit of the Pope to the hospital of Spirito Santo.

590. Inscription, etc., same as above.
TU. DOMINUS. ET. MAGISTER.
Washing the feet on Holy Thursday.

591. Inscription, etc., same as above.
BAPTISTERIO. LIBERIANO. ERECTO. DEDICATO.
Baptismal font at St. Mary Major.

592. Inscription, etc., same as above.
TU. DOMINUS. ET. MAGISTER.
Washing the feet on Holy Thursday.

593. Inscription, etc., same as above.
DEIPARAE. DICATUM. IN. ANTRO. GINGUINI. MONTIS.
Chapel erected at Genga, the Pope's native place.

594. Inscription, etc., same as above.
IN. FORTI. TURRIS. IN. TUA. FIDE. FORTIOR. ORBIS.
The figure of "Religion," the world in one hand, the cross in the other.

PIUS VIII. 1829 to 1830.

595. Pius VIII., Pon. Max., Anno. I.
TU. DOMINUS. ET. MAGISTER.
Washing the feet, etc.

596. Inscription, etc., same as above.
S. SEDIS. LATERANEN. POSSESSIO.
The Pope at St. John Lateran.

597. Inscription, etc., same as above.
LACRIMÆ. PATRIS. LÆTITIA. FILIORUM.
The figure of "Religion," the cross in one hand, the chalice in the other.

598. Inscription, etc., same as above.
> BENEMERENTI.

599. Inscription, etc., same as above.
> BENEMERENTI.
> Larger size.

600. Inscription, etc., same as above.
> AUDITORIBUS. ARCHIGYMN. ROMANI.

601. Inscription, etc., same as above.
> ACADEMIIS. ARCHIGYMN. ROMANI.

602. Inscription, etc., same as above.
> TU. DOMINUS. ET. MAGISTER.
> Washing of the feet.

603. Inscription, etc., same as above.
> JUSTITIA. ET. PAX. OSCULATÆ. SUNT.
> "Justice," with the sword; "Peace," with the olive branch.

GREGORIUS XVI. 1831 to 1846.

604. Gregorius XVI., Pont. Max., Anno I.
> HÆC. EST. VICTORIA. QUÆ. VINCIT. MUNDUM.
> Three crowns of olive. "Victoria."

605. Inscription, etc., same as above.
> GREGORIO. XVI, PONT. MAX. ARTIUM. ET. SCIENTIARUM. PATRONO, OPTIMO.

606. Inscription, etc., same as above.
> TU. DOMINUS. ET. MAGISTER.
> Washing of the feet.

607. Inscription, etc., same as above.
> BENEMERENTI.

608. Inscription, etc., same as above.
> DEXTERA. DOMINI. FECIT. VIRTUTEM.
> Figure of " Religion " trampling on the hydra.

609. Inscription, etc., same as above.
> BENEMERENTI.
> Supported by two little angels.

610. Inscription, etc., same as above.
> BENEMERENTI.

611. Inscription, etc., same as above.
> TU. DOMINUS. ET. MAGISTER.
> Washing of the feet.

612. Inscription, etc., same as above.
> S. SEDIS. LATERANEN. POSSESS.
> Solemn "possession."

613. Inscription, etc., same as above.
> NON. PRÆOALEBUNT. ADVERSUS. EAM.
> Rome triumphant by the dispersion of the enemies of the Holy See.

614. Inscription, etc., same as above.
> ACCADEMIIS, Etc.

616. Inscription, etc., same as above.
> TU. DOMINUS. ET. MAGISTER.
> Washing of the feet.

617. Inscription, etc., same as above.
> PACIS. ET. RELIGIONIS. AMOR.
> Figure of " Peace " and " Religion.

618. Inscription, etc., same as above.
TU. DOMINUS. ET. MAGISTER.
Washing of the feet.

619. Inscription, etc., same as above.
CATILLO. MONTE. AD. ANIENEM. AVERTENDUM. PERFOSSO. ELVIONUM. CLADIBUS. OCCURRIT.
View of Monte Catillo in Tivoli.

620. Inscription, etc., same as above.
BONO. PUBLICO. LEGIBUS. OPTIMIS. CONSULIT. REM. NUMMARIAM. CONSTITUIT.
Reform of the finances.

621. Inscription, etc., same as above.
TU. DOMINUS. ET. MAGISTER.
Washing the feet.

622. Inscription, etc., same as above.
MONUM. VET. SERVATA.
Temple of Antonine and Fanstina changed into St. Lawrence in Miranda.

623. Inscription, etc., same as above.
TIBURTES. CATILLO. PERFORATO. INDUCTO. ANIENE. SERVATI. MDCCCXXXV.
Two views of Monte Catillo in Tivoli.

624. Inscription, etc., same as above.
OPUS. BIENNIO. INCHOATUM. ANNO. MDCCCXXXV. PERFOSSA. CATILLI. RUPE.
Same as No. 623, smaller size.

625. Inscription, etc., same as above.
TU. DOMINUS. ET. MAGISTER.
Washing of the feet.

626. Inscription, etc., same as above.
12. GIUGNO. 1836.
Premium to the corps of firemen.

627. Inscription, etc., same as above.
CENTUMCELL. URBE. AMPLIFICATA.
City and port of Civitavecchia.

628. Inscription, etc., same as above.
TU. DOMINUS. ET. MAGISTER.
Washing of the feet.

629. Inscription, etc., same as above.
SACRARIUM. PAULINUM. RESTITUIT.
The Pauline chapel restored.

630. Inscription, etc., same as above.
MUSEUM. GREG. EX. MON. ETRUSCIS.
The Etruscan Museum.

631. Inscription, etc., same as above.
NOVUM. ÆD. VATICAN. DECUS. 1837.
Figure of "Rome" surrounded by specimens from Egypt.

632. Inscription, etc., same as above.
BASILIC. S. PAULI. EX. INCENDIO. XV. JUL. 1823.
Interior of the Basilica of St. Paul, destroyed by fire.

633. Inscription, etc., same as above.
TU. DOMINUS. ET. MAGISTER.
Washing of the feet.

634. Inscription, etc., same as above.
PORTICU. ERUTIS. SOLO. VEJENTI. COLUMNIS. ERUCTA.
New building for the Post Office.

635. Inscription, etc., same as above.
>TU. DOMINUS. ET. MAGISTER.
>Washing of the feet.

636. Inscription, etc., same as above.
>MIRABILIS, DEUS. IN. SANCTIS. SUIS.
>Canonization of St. Alphonsus de'Liguori, of St. Francis of Jerome, of St. John Joseph of the Cross, of St. Pacificus of Severino, and St. Veronica Juliani, in 1839.

637. Inscription, etc., same as above.
>MUSEUM. GREG. EX. MON. ÆGYPTIIS.
>Interior of the Egyptian Museum.

638. Inscription, etc., same as above.
>TU. DOMINUS. ET. MAGISTER.
>Washing of the feet.

639. Inscription, etc., same as above.
>CAUSA. NOSTRÆ. LÆTITIÆ.
>Bust of the Blessed Virgin

640. Inscription, etc., same as above.
>UBI. INDEDICA. LOCO. LIGNA., ETC.
>View of the new building near the Ripetta on the Tiber, Rome.

641. Inscription, etc., same as above.
>INSTITUIT. GUARDIA. CIVICA. 1649.
>Premium Medal.

642. Inscription, etc., same as above.
>BENEFICENTIA. PUBLICA.
>Refers to his care of the poor.

643. Inscription, etc., same as above.
>TU. DOMINUS. ET. MAGISTER.
>Washing of the feet.

644. Inscription, etc., same as above.
>DUCTUS. ACQUÆ. CLAUDIÆ. DILAPSIS, Etc.
>View of the Claudian monument of the "Porta Maggiore."

645. Inscription, etc., same as above.
>TU. DOMINUS. ET. MAGISTER.
>Washing of the feet.

646. Inscription, etc., same as above.
>ANCONITANA. RESTITUTA. NOVIS. OPERIBUS. MUNITA. 1842.
>View of the Fortress of Ancona.

647. Inscription, etc., same as above.
>DOMO. HOSPITALI. MICHAELIANA. COMMODIS, Etc.
>View of the Apostolic Hospice of St. Michael and of the Ripa Grande, Rome.

648. Inscription, etc., same as above.
>TU. DOMINUS. FT. MAGISTER.
>Washing of the feet.

649. Inscription, etc., same as above.
>PORTU. TERRACINÆ. SALUTARI. CIVIBUS, Etc.
>View of the new Port and Canal of Terracina

650. Inscription, etc., same as above.
>TU. DOMINUS. ET. MAGISTER.
>Washing of the feet.

651. Inscription, etc., same as above.
VALETUDINARIO. INCURABILIUM. AD. S. JACOBI. IN. AUGUSTA. RESTITUTO. AMPLIATO. 1844.
View of the Hospital of St. James, Incurables.

652. Inscription, etc , same as above.
TU. DOMINUS. ET. MAGISTER.
Washing of the feet.

653. Inscription, etc., same as above.
ÆQUATO. GALLORI. JUGO. PONTE, Etc., 1843.
View of the Bridge at Galloro.

554. Inscription, etc., same as above.
TU. DOMINUS. ET. MAGISTER.
Washing of the feet.

PIUS IX. 1846 to 1878.

655. PIUS IX. P. M. EL. DIE. XVII. COR. DIE. XXI. JUNII. ANNO. 1846.
ROMÆ. PARENTES. ARBITRIQUE. GENTIUM.
Bust of the Holy Apostles St. Peter and St. Paul.

656. Inscription, etc., same as above.
BENEMERENTI.

657. Similar to 656.

658. Similar to 656.

659. Similar to 656.

660. Inscription, etc., same as above.
AUDITORIBUS. ARCHIGYMNASII. ROMANI.

661. Inscription, etc., same as above.
ACCADEMIIS. ARCHIGY. ROMANI.

662. Inscription, etc., same as above.
SACRÆ. SEDIS. LATER. POSSESS.
The solemn " Possession" of the Pontiff.

663. Inscription, etc., same as above.
EGO. DOMINUS. ET. MAGISTER.
Washing of the feet.

664. Inscription, etc., same as above.
BASILIC. S. PAULI. EX. INCENDIO. XV. JUL.
Interior of the Church of St. Paul, destroyed by fire.

665. Inscription, etc., same as above.
CAUSA. NOSTRÆ. LÆTITIÆ.
Bust of the Blessed Virgin with "halo."

666. Inscription, etc., same as above.
DIE. XXV. APRILIS. 1847.
Premium Medal.

667. Inscription, etc., same as above.
BASILIC. VATICANÆ. DECUS. ADDITUM. 1847.
Statues of the Holy Apostles.

668. Inscription, etc., same as above.
LEGATIONE. PERFUNCTIS. AD. PIUM. IX. P. M. ELECTUM. NOMINE. MAGNI. TURC. DOMINI. AN. 1847.
A number of distinguished personages accompanying the Ambassador Extraordinary of the "Sublime Porte."

669. Inscription, etc., same as above.
IN. LABORIBUS. A. JUVENTUTE. MEA.
The Holy Family.

670. Inscription, etc., same as above.
EGO. DOMINUS. ET. MAGISTER.
Washing of the feet.

671. Inscription, etc., same as above.
MUNICIPAL. IN. URBE. RESTITUTOR.
Moses gives to the heads of the Tribes of Israel the Municipal Laws.

672. Inscription, etc., same as above.
CAUSA. NOSTRÆ. LÆTITIA.
Bust of the Blessed Virgin.

673. Inscription, etc., same as above.
CAJETA. IN. CŒNA. DOMINI.
EGO. DOMINUS. ET. MAGISTER.
Washing of the feet at Gaeta.

674. Inscription, etc., same as above.
PIUS IX. PONT. MAX. ROMÆ. RESTITUTUS. CATHOLICIS. ARMIS. COLLATIS. AN. 1849.
Premium Medal for foreign troops.

675. Inscription, etc., same as above.
CASERTÆ. IN. CŒNA. DOMINI.
Washing of the feet in Caserta.

676. Inscription, etc., same as above.
QUEM. SEDE. ROMANA. IMPIE. EXTURBATUM. PROVINCIA. CAMPANEÆ. INGEMEBAT., Etc.
The province of Frosinone, for the happy return of the Pope to his States.

677. Inscription, etc., same as above.
PRINCIPI. EXOPTATO. A. DIUTINO. FERDINANDI REGIS. SICILIÆ., Etc.
The province of Rome.

678. Inscription, etc., same as above.
PIO IX. PONT. MAX. FAUSTE. FELICITER. REDEUNTI.
The Roman Nobles.

679. Inscription, etc., same as above.
PRECE. URBEM. LUSTRANTI AN. 1850. A. REDITU. PRINCIPIS. CLARIORA. NITENT.
The return to Rome of the Sovereign Pontiff.

680. Inscription, etc., same as above.
FIDELITATI.
Premium Medal for fidelity to the Holy Apostolic See.

681. Inscription, etc., same as above.
DIRUPTUS. EST. DRACO. ET. DIXIT. DANIEL. ECCE. QUEM. COLEBATIS.
The Prophet Daniel.

682. Inscription, etc., same as above.
EGO. DOMINUS. ET. MAGISTER.
Washing of the feet.

683. Inscription, etc., same as above.
IN. URBEM. REVERSUS. PASTOR. NON. ULTOR.
The Dove with an Olive branch.

684. Inscription, etc., same as above.
FRANCIÆ. MILITES. AEGROTANTES. A. PIO IX. PONT. MAX. VISITATI., Etc.
The Pelican.

— 95 —

685. Inscription, etc., same as above.
ALBANO. ET. ARICCIA. PONTE. CONJUNCTIS. 1851.
View of the Bridge of Ariccia.

686. Inscription, etc., same as above.
VOLONTARIO.
Medal for the Pontifical Soldiers.

687. Pius IX. Pont. Max. Anno. VI.
EGO. DOMINUS. ET. MAGISTER.
Washing of the feet.

688. Inscription, etc., same as above.
ARTIUM. INDUSTRIÆ. ET. AGRICULTURÆ.
PREMIUM.
Premium Medal for the Department of Commerce and Agriculture.

689. Inscription, etc., same as above, but smaller.

690. Inscription, etc., same as above.
VIA. APPIA. RESTITUTA.
View of the ancient "Via Appia."

691. Inscription, etc., same as above.
OPTIMO. PRINCIPI. ÆDES. ÆRARIO. PUBLICO. Etc.
Visit of the Pope to the Department of Finances.

692. Inscription, etc., same as above.
EGO. DOMINUS. ET. MAGISTER.
Washing of the feet.

693. Inscription, etc., same as above.
PIUS. IX. P. M. BASILICÆ. LATERAN. ALTARE.
MAX. AD. VETEREM. FORMAM. RESTITUIT.
AC. SPLENDIDIORI. CULTU. INSTAURAVIT.
View of the "Confession" in St. John Lateran.

694. Inscription, etc., same as above.
MUSEUM. IN. ÆDIBUS. LATERAN. AUCTUM. AN. 1853.
   A wing of the new Lateran Museum.

695. Inscription, etc., same as above.
PASCE. OVES. MEAS.
   Our Lord and St. Peter. Alludes to the founding of the "Seminario Pio."

696. Inscription, etc., same as above.
EGO. DOMINUS. ET. MAGISTER.
   Washing of the feet.

697. Inscription, etc., same as above.
SINITE. PARVULOS. VENIRE. AD. ME.
   Infants' Home, Rome.

698. Inscription, etc., same as above.
PROVIDENTIA. OPTIMI. PRINCIPIS. ARICCIÆ. CLIVO. PERICULO. SUBLATO.
   The viaduct of Ariccia.

699. Inscription, etc., same as above.
EGO. DOMINUS. ET. MAGISTER.
   Washing of the feet.

700. Inscription, etc., same as above.
AD. SANCTI. SPIRITUS. LUE. LABORANTES. INVISIT. XI. KAL. SEPT. 1854.
   Visit of the Pope to the hospital of "Santo Spirito."

701. Inscription, etc., same as above.
PORTÆ. PIÆ. TURRIM. FULMEN. LABEFECERAT.
   View of the "Porta Pia" restored.

702. Inscription, etc., same as above.
PIUS. IX. PONT. MAX. PATER. INDULGENTISSIMUS. SENATORI. ET. CONSERVATORIBUS. URBIS. ANNO. REP. SAL. 1854. LUE. ASIANA. IN. URBEM. GRASSANTE. DE. CIVIUM. INCOLUMITATE. PRÆCLARE. MERITIS.

Premium medal to the municipality of Rome on occasion of the cholera.

703. Inscription, etc., same as above.
EGO DOMINUS. ET. MAGISTER.

Washing of the feet.

704. Inscription, etc., same as above.
SINE. LABE. CONCEPTA.

Definition of the dogma of the IMMACULATE CONCEPTION.

705. Inscription, etc., same as above.
Similar to No. 688.

706. Inscription, etc., same as above.
IN. DITIONE. PONTIFICIA. FERRÆ. VIÆ. COMMODITAS. ROMA. TUSCULUM. PRIMUM. IN. DUCTA. 1856.

In commemoration of the opening of the railroad from Rome to Frascati.

707. Inscription, etc., same as above.
PRÆMIUM. PRÆSTANTIORIBUS. AD. DRAMATA. CONCINNANDA. STUDIO. CIVILIS. MORIS. COMMENDATIONE. VIRTUTIS.

Medal as a premium for dramatists.

708. Inscription, etc., same as above.
>   EGO. DOMINUS. ET. MAGISTER.
>   Washing of the feet.

709. Inscription, etc., same as above.
>   BENEMERENTI.
>   A very small medal for a decoration.

710. Inscription, etc., same as above.
>   FELIX. BONONIA.
>   The Pope visits this province of his States.

711. Inscription, etc., same as above.
OB. PRÆSENTIAM. SUMMI. ANTISTITIS. RELIGION.
>   View of the church of the " Madonna di San Lucoa," in Bologna.

712. Inscription, etc., same as above.
>   FERREA. VIA. ROMAM. PROVINCIIS. JUNGI. CURAVIT.
>   Figure of the railroads of the pontifical States.

713. Inscription, etc., same as above.
>   BONONIENSEM. OFFICINAM. INVISEBAT.
>   View of the pontifical mint at Bologna.

714. Inscription, etc., same as above.
PATRI. PERAMANTI. EXOPTATISSIMO. E. LUSTRATIONE. IN. URBEM. REVERTENTI. PROVINCIA. ROMANA. 1857.
>   The province of Rome on the return of the Holy Father to Rome.

715. Inscription, etc., same as above.
OB. ERECT. COLUMN. CONC. IMMAC. B. V. M. DICATA.
The "Immaculate Conception" on the column erected in the "Piazza di Spagna."

716. Inscription, etc., same as above.
CENTUMCELLAS. INVISENTI. QUOD. IMMUNITATIBUS. CONFIRMATIS. VIAM. FERRATAM. LUSTRAVIT. CIVITATIS. AMPLIANDÆ. FACULTATEM. DEDIT. CENTUMCELLENSES.

717. Inscription, etc., same as above.
TEMPLI. EXTRUENDI. CHRISTI. MARTYRIBUS. ALEXANDRO. PAPÆ. EVENTIO. ET. THEODULO. PRESB. PRIMUM. FUNDAM. LAPIDEM. VITE. POSUIT. 1857.
Medal commemorating the founding of the Church of St. Alexander outside of the "Porta Pia."

718. Inscription, etc., same as above.
EGO. DOMINUS. ET. MAGISTER.
Washing of the feet.

719. Inscription, etc., same as above.
PROVINCIARUM. LUSTRATIO. 1857.
The visitation of his Provinces by the Pope.

720. Inscription, etc., same as above.
EGO. DOMINUS. ET. MAGISTER.
Washing of the feet.

721. Inscription, etc., same as above.
BENEMERENTI.
Premium Medal for military trophies.

722. Inscription, etc., same as above.
PORTAM. URBIS. IN. JANICULI. VERTICE. RESTI-
TUIT. ORNAVIT. 1854.
View of the "Porta Pancrazio."

723. Inscription, etc., same as above.
BENEMERENTI.
Medal for Civil Officers.

724. Inscription, etc., same as above.
EGO. DOMINUS. ET. MAGISTER.
Washing of the feet.

725. Inscription, etc., same as above.
MULTITUDINIS. CREDENTIUM. COR. UNUM. ET.
ANIMA. UNA.
Medal struck at Easter, 1860.

726. Inscription, etc., same as above.
FIDEI. REGULA. ECCLES. FUNDAMENTUM.
The Chair of St. Peter in Rome.

727. Inscription, etc., same as above.
EGO. DOMINUS. ET. MAGISTER.
Washing of the feet.

728. Inscription, etc., same as above.
DEUS. MEUS. CONCLUDAT. ORA. LEONUM.
Daniel in the lions' den.

729. Inscription, etc., same as above.
EGO. DOMINUS. ET. MAGISTER.
Washing of the feet.

730. Inscription, etc., same as above.
BASILICAM. PAULI. APOST. AB. INCENDIO. REFECTAM. SOLEMNI. RITU. CONSECRAVIT. 1854.
View of the interior of St. Paul's, Rome.

731. Inscription, etc., same as above.
PETRI. INOPIAM. CHRISTIANI. STIPE. SUSTENTANT.
St. Peter receives alms offered as Peter's pence.

732. Inscription, etc., same as above.
EGO. DOMINUS. ET. MAGISTER.
Washing of the feet.

733. Inscription, etc., same as above.
TERTIA. SÆCULARIA. FESTA. A. CONCILIO. ABSOLUTO. TRIDENTO. 1863.
Medal commemorating the third centenary of the Council of Trent.

734. Inscription, etc., same as above.
ANNO. 1863 TRIDENTINI. CONCILII. TERCENTENARIUS.
Same as preceding but smaller.

735. Inscription, etc., same as above.
NICOTIANIS. FOLIIS. ELABORANDIS. OFFICINAM. APTIOREM. A. SOLO. EXTRUXIT. 1863.
On the reverse, view of a manufactory of tobacco in Rome.

736. Inscription, etc., same as above.
EGO. DOMINUS. ET. MAGISTER.
Washing of the feet.

737. Inscription, etc., same as above.

ANNO. MDCCCLXIV.

View of "Porta Pia."

738. Inscription, etc., same as above.

EGO. DOMINUS. ET. MAGISTER.

Washing of the feet.

739. Inscription, etc., same as above.

COHORTI. VIGILUM. URBAN. EXPERIMENTO. PUBLICE. EXHIBITO.

Premium for The Corps of Firemen.

740. Inscription, etc., same as above.

TEMPLUM. S. LAURENTII. M. RESTITUIT. ORNAVIT. 1865.

View of the Church of St. Lawrence outside the walls of Rome.

741. Inscription, etc., same as above.

EGO. DOMINUS. ET. MAGISTER.

Washing of the feet.

742. Inscription, etc., same as above.

HOSPITIUM. DEMENTIBUS. CURAND. COMMODIS. INSTAURATUM. AMPLIATUM.

743. Inscription, etc., same as above.

EXEMPLUM. DEDI. VOBIS.

Our Lord washes St. Peter's feet.

744. Inscription, etc., same as above.

PRINCEPS. APOSTOLORUM. DOCTOR. GENTIUM. ISTI. SUNT. TRIUMPHATORES. ET. AMICI. DEI.

Alludes to the solemn 18th centenary of the Holy Apostles, 1867.

745. Inscription, etc., same as above.

ROMÆ. PARENTES. ARBITRIQUE. GENTIUM. S. PETRUS. S. PAULUS. 1867.

Alludes to the same.

746. Inscription, etc., same as above.

ADSCENSU. COMMODIORE. AD. COLLEM. QUIRINALEM. APERTO. EXORNATO.

View of the new approach to the Quirinal.

747. Inscription, etc., same as above.

OB. CHRISTIANÆ. CHARITATIS. OFFICIA. LUE. ASIANA. CORREPTIS. EXHIBITA.

Medal for those who cared for the cholera patients in 1867.

748. Inscription, etc., same os above.

FIDEI. ET. VIRTUTI. HINC. VICTORIA.

Commemoration of the victory at Mentana. Military decoration.

749. Inscription' etc., same as above.

EXEMPLUM. DEDI. VOBIS.

Our Lord washes St. Peter's feet.

750. Inscription, etc., same as above.
> PORTICUS. DOM. PONT. M. VAT. EXSCULPTA.
> The Gallery "Piana" in the Vatican.

751. Inscription, etc., same as above.
> Washing of the feet.

752. Inscription, etc., same as above.
> IN. CŒM. URB. AD. AGRUM. VERAN.

Monument erected in the Cemetery of St. Lawrence commemorating the soldiers slain at Mentana.

www.ingramcontent.com/pod-product-compliance
Lightning Source LLC
Chambersburg PA
CBHW021947160426
43195CB00011B/1254